GW01319600

Great Australian
BUSHFIRE
STORIES

Great Australian
BUSHFIRE
STORIES

Ian Mannix

ABC
Books

Published by ABC Books for the
AUSTRALIAN BROADCASTING CORPORATION
GPO Box 9994 Sydney NSW 2001

Copyright © Ian Mannix 2008

First published October 2008

All rights reserved. No part of this publication
may be reproduced, stored in a retrieval system or
transmitted in any form or by any means, electronic,
mechanical, photocopying, recording or otherwise,
without the prior written permission of the Australian
Broadcasting Corporation.

ISBN 978 0 7333 2397 3

Cover design by Josh Durham at Design by Committee
Cover images by Newspix
Typeset in 11.5 on 20pt AdobeCaslon Regular by Kirby Jones
Printed in Australia by Griffin Press, Adelaide

10 9 8 7 6 5 4 3 2 1

DEDICATION

On 21 January 1997, an arsonist lit five fires in the heavily timbered Dandenong Ranges just east of Melbourne, and they erupted into a major blaze. Forty-one houses were burnt in a matter of hours.

Jennifer Lindroth, 26, her husband Graham, 24, died, along with their neighbour, 50-year-old Genevieve Erin.

Jennifer's mother, Jacqui Bell, recalls, 'I rang and told them there were fires in the hills, but there was no smoke and no fire in their area. The fire wasn't there at all. But they put their fire plan into action, and were packing the car and getting ready to leave. Jennifer called me and said she was scared, as it had gone suddenly black everywhere. I told her to leave immediately. At the last minute they decided to stay for some reason, and they went back into the cellar of their house, which was also something they'd planned. I was hoping they might have curled up into a little ball together, but in fact they died apart.'

Since that day I have been asking. 'What Can ABC Local Radio do to help people confronted by bushfires?' This book is dedicated to all those who have shared that goal.

CONTENTS

INTRODUCTION

WE'VE MADE IT TOO HARD TO STAY HOME

Bushfire is an important part of Australian mythology. Whether we live in cities, towns or in the bush, its menace is seared into our brains from birth: toddlers learn the word 'burny' as a threat very early, and we are constantly warned against playing with matches. Every summer our TV screens show us sheets of flame engulfing houses or bushland, with the tired, grimy faces of bushfire victims testifying to the terror of the ordeal they have just endured.

The media have convinced us that bushfire is uncontrollable and extreme. We have come to believe that firefighters are brave beyond normal capacity, that only heroes risk their lives to save neighbours or unknown families from burning homes. The message is that only the strongest are able to confront the horror of bushfire.

Yet bushfires can be survived, and property can mostly be defended. Considering what a threat fire poses to communities around Australia, this is a message that has been poorly understood. One Queensland government report states simply: 'The best way to handle bushfires is to ensure that people get over the perceptual characterisation of wildfire as a terrifying aberration.'

Not everybody needs to heed this message. Indeed, it could be argued that fire generally is not something we are especially afraid of. Without fear we reach into combustion heaters to place wood in the right spot on a blazing fire; we shift wood to a better spot in a campfire; most people casually brush embers from their clothes; tradesmen are not worried by the sparks of an angle grinder. We know that fire should be respected but not feared.

Australians living in remote and rural communities understand very well that bushfires are facts of nature that simply have to be dealt with. They know they cannot rely on a convoy of fire trucks with quantities of water, nor on well-trained volunteers with cool heads. But a large proportion of the population, while they may fear the possibility of bushfire, are surprisingly complacent about preparing for it, often believing that fire and police authorities will always have enough time to warn and evacuate people. Some try to prepare but legal, environmental and political factors may prevent proper neighbour or community preparation. Some make preparations but receive insufficient accurate and timely warnings; some try to face the threat alone; and some believe they have the courage to face the threat but, if the fire is worse than they imagined, they may panic.

The complexity of bushfire and the vagaries of human behaviour present emergency authorities around Australia with a dilemma: in case of danger, should people be encouraged to stay at home and defend their property, or should they be encouraged to abandon it?

The question seems a simple one, yet it certainly is not. Firefighting authorities hedge their bets: some people should leave early, some should shelter in their homes if directly threatened by a bushfire. Sometimes whole streets are instructed to evacuate their homes in the face of bushfires, and those with fire plans are also questioned, sometimes at the very last minute, about their capacity to stay and defend their property. Instructions may be poorly expressed – who should heed these messages? What does 'leaving early' mean? It is difficult to understand the implications of such advice when the threat of fire is imminent and clear thought is almost impossible.

There are many cases where people have chosen not to heed the authorities' advice, yet have survived. In 2003 hundreds of

Canberra houses were burned down when a state of emergency was declared: home owners were ordered to leave whole suburbs. However, Richard Stanton and a neighbour in Duffy stayed at home, remained cool-headed when all around were panicking, and helped to save five homes. On New Year's Day 2004 Charles and Kathie Smith at Phegans Bay, near Gosford, New South Wales, were told to evacuate their home by police; ten men left but the Smiths quickly arranged for a small group to stay and protect the properties in their street. During the 2006 bushfires in the Australian Alps, twelve people in Gaffneys Creek refused to leave when they knew they would face the fires alone; they saved their own homes as well as unoccupied houses.

These people understood fire and their own ability to cope: these factors alone were often enough to save their homes and properties.

Tasmanian Fire Commissioner John Gledhill is renowned for encouraging people to take responsibility for learning about bushfire rather than relying on specialist agencies. He believes that emergency services have unintentionally served to disempower people in the community, encouraging citizens to believe emergency services can deal with any threat. 'But there is a point where it is beyond the resources of emergency services to assist people,' he says. 'People have to take responsibility and look after each other: there has to be responsibility for leadership. It's amazing what people can do if they are well led.' This involves making decisions about whether to abandon property or to stay and defend it.

'Preparation is the key to the strategy, and people have to be properly prepared,' he says. 'It is difficult to know when to leave a property faced with a bushfire threat. Ideally residents should leave before there is any threat to their area. But we know that going early is not always practical, and we also know that sometimes there will not be time to evacuate. Making a decision to let a home burn is traumatic.

'Maybe we convey the danger too well, or make it sound too hard to stay.' In an attempt to counter public lack of knowledge, the Tasmania Fire Service has issued 40,000 CDs to citizens, explaining the elements of fire prevention and effective preparation. Community fire units in other states provide similar services, and the CSIRO has disseminated a great deal of information about the behaviour of bushfires.

Of Australia's firefighting staff and volunteers, John Gledhill says: 'We train them well, they have confidence in their equipment, systems they can rely on and other people there with them. And we lead them to fires gently.'

Timely and accurate warning systems are of course vital. ABC Local Radio broadcasts early warnings, provided of course that they are given reliable information by bushfire agencies. But these agencies sometimes tell the community there is a problem only when a fire is already out of control. Fire and police agencies need to be in touch with fire-prone communities through days of total fire ban, even when fires do not ignite, thus building awareness that leads to accountability.

Agencies are also building on their knowledge of human behaviour. John Handmer, Director of the Centre for Risk and Community Safety at RMIT University in Melbourne, has noticed a worrying new trend in bushfire survival: mothers and children, encouraged to flee their homes while fathers stay to defend their property, are dying in car accidents, while men survive. 'Families may underestimate their ability to cope,' he says. 'Many are unwilling to recognise that children, even as young as about ten, can provide substantial help in defending a house in relative safety.'

Residents threatened with bushfire, however, may cling to certain beliefs that are problematic. The first thing many people do when threatened by a bushfire is to get on the roof and fill the gutters with water. It's an understandable action: embers often land in the gutters and begin burning the rafters, and they can be easily doused. However, John Gledhill thinks this should be done carefully. 'In the Canberra fires, there were more injuries caused by falls from ladders and roofs than from burns,' he says.

Many people live in fire-prone areas because they love the environment. 'Eucalypts are a fire problem,' says Gledhill. 'But that doesn't mean we need to cut down trees. Fire is not transmitted in treetops without an accompanying ground fire.

Trees will flare but if there is nothing on the ground to burn, that is all that will happen.' A bigger problem is the common suburban love of pine bark and woodchips. 'We're inviting fire into our suburbs,' he says.

It is well recognised, of course, that many people who live in bushfire-prone regions know how to defend their property. They are fit, knowledgeable about fire behaviour, love and understand the natural environment, and have time and resources for preparation and defence. When fires threaten, those who resist the danger best are people who have already thought about the best ways of safeguarding the welfare of children, pets and elderly or frail relatives. Gledhill puts the matter succinctly: 'Get the facts, focus on the event, don't think the worst, don't put yourself down, take one step at a time.' Ultimately the message is about people, not fire: people have the fundamental responsibility for their own safety.

The communities and individuals in this book have all learned from their confrontation with 'the red steer'. By allowing us to see their personal responses to Australia's summer menace, they have allowed us to understand better how to protect ourselves, our families and our communities.

ONE

THIRTY-EIGHT-WEEKS PREGNANT

In 2000 Richard and Sonia Stanton, with their baby daughter Emma, moved into 67 Warragamba Avenue, Duffy, on the western side of Canberra. In some ways the Stantons were a typical Canberra professional couple: Sonia an endocrinologist and Richard a policy manager with the forest and wood products industry. They liked the house because of its peaceful setting. On the other side of Warragamba Avenue, and visible from the Stantons' lounge room, was a pine plantation stretching all the way to Mt Stromlo, five kilometres away.

'I was always conscious that bushfire was a possibility here,' says Richard, a former volunteer with the NSW Rural Fire

Brigade at Hornsby in Sydney's northern suburbs. 'We are on the very edge of the suburb and I always thought that if any houses were at risk, ours was. But I did think we were far enough away from the forest to manage that risk.'

Richard, who had lived in Canberra since 1985, knew that bushfires were part of the area's history. In December 1951, 450 hectares of pine trees at Mt Stromlo had been burned and several buildings belonging to the Observatory there had been destroyed. That fire had claimed the lives of two people and property including two houses, forty farm buildings, six bridges, three vehicles and several hundred kilometres of fencing.

The Stantons had had vicarious experience of bushfire, too. On Christmas Day 2001, fire, as well as severely damaging areas of pine forest and native landscape west of Lake Burley Griffin, had threatened Government House and the Mint. Richard sent Sonia, his sister Ruth and one-year-old Emma to a friend's home while he stayed behind to protect their property. Fortunately, the fires did not reach them.

'I always felt things would be all right if I had the basic firefighting equipment and time to prepare,' says Richard. 'But I think I was lazy about longer-term planning. Sonia and I didn't sit down and discuss what we would do if there was a bushfire near us.' The Stantons kept the vegetation around their house to a minimum; though two large eucalypts on the nature strip in front cast a little shade, the driveway was concrete and the area between the front steps and the road was paved. They kept the garden tidy and the lawn mowed and Richard cleaned out the gutters a couple of times a year. They had overalls and face masks, and made sure that the hoses would stretch all the way around the house.

On Wednesday 8 January 2003, lightning strikes from an electrical storm ignited fires in the Namadgi National Park fifty kilometres southwest of Canberra and in the Brindabella Ranges about thirty kilometres to the west. The storm brought no rain, and the fires raged out of control, though residents of Canberra were told not to be unduly concerned. However, on 18 January, a scorchingly hot and windy Saturday, the fires merged, creating a front thirty-five kilometres long. Richard became increasingly anxious.

'We went to Weston Creek to do the weekly shopping and I told Sonia that we needed to hurry up,' he recalls. 'It was a bad fire day and I wanted to be home keeping an eye on things.' Sonia, who was thirty-eight-weeks pregnant, cannot have relished walking quickly through the paved supermarket car park with a small child and an impatient husband.

'We got home around lunchtime and discovered that the fires in the Brindabellas were raging out of control twenty kilometres from the suburbs. Sonia and Emma went inside for lunch, and I went outside and cleaned up. We had some leftover fence palings on the western side of the house, and I moved them right down the backyard. I checked the hoses and moved the rubbish bins away from the house.'

On the 1pm news, Richard and Sonia were alarmed to hear that the fire service in the rural areas to the west had stopped fighting the fire and had withdrawn to property protection. 'They said it in a low-key way and I think they made the point that it was only an issue for the rural properties. To me that meant they had given up and acknowledged they couldn't stop the fires. I thought, Well, if that's happening, the fires could get here. But I didn't think about when that could happen.'

Richard advised Sonia to pack a bag and leave. 'If she hadn't been pregnant and we hadn't had a young child, I would have asked her to stay. But I thought it was important for her to be close to a hospital if she needed one; the fire might have trapped her in the suburb.

'She only prepared her hospital bag: she wasn't taking any prized possessions. I was pretty confident I could protect the house.'

Soon afterwards, Richard took Emma for a drive. 'She had a sleep every afternoon and it was easier to settle her down in the car. Besides, I wanted to see exactly where the fires were, and check for smoke.'

Meanwhile, Sonia stayed at home and prepared the interior of the house while she listened for fire updates on the radio. 'I filled the sinks and both bathtubs and put towels in each tub,' she says.

'I wasn't sure why Richard might use them, but if the worst came to the worst he'd have towels already wet.

'I shut all the doors and windows and made sure they weren't locked. I tried to block off all the openings but didn't put towels under the doors. If Richard was running, I wanted to be sure he wouldn't trip over anything.

'I wasn't sure what to do with the windows. I had heard you needed to tape them and not to leave any soft furnishings near them. But I wasn't sure how much effort to put into the preparations, so I moved the soft furnishings away from the walls on the western side of the house.

'I took the curtains down so there was nothing flammable near the window. The two bathrooms on the western side of the house had vents at the top of the windows, so I dunked a hand towel and soaked it and stuffed it into the holes, thinking no embers would come through if it was blocked and wet.

'Afterwards I realised they would have lasted about three milliseconds with that intense heat. And I should have placed some torches in the house for Richard, but I didn't think about that because it was two o'clock in the afternoon of a blazing hot day.'

Sonia was calm as she waited for Richard to return, reassured because she couldn't see any smoke. But she would have felt the wind pick up and change direction from north to northwest and, though she did not know it, there was smoke nearby.

Out driving with Emma, Richard saw it. 'I drove up the street, then turned round, and for the first time I could see a huge column of smoke, enormous cumulonimbus clouds out to the west. I couldn't tell where its base was because it was so big. The rest of the sky was clear and blue. I thought, That's not good.'

Richard drove home. Emma was asleep, and it seemed sensible to put her to bed. 'I didn't want her to wake up. I put on my overalls and said I was going out to make sure everything was okay outside and I'd block the gutters.' Richard cannot remember whether he and Sonia discussed the smoke cloud and its implications. Perhaps they felt the threat would not be so deadly if they didn't put it into words, and there were practical matters to attend to. Richard blocked the downpipes with nappies and filled the gutters with water, and put a soaker hose on at the front of the house. He then decided to visit neighbours and help if he could. Several were away, but one neighbour, Greg, was hosing his home down; one elderly couple were preparing to leave. Friends in one nearby house were away, so Richard climbed onto their roof and began to clean up their guttering.

From his vantage point, he could see the cloud of smoke above the pine plantation. 'I knew it had to be reasonably close, but I still had no idea where the fire was,' he says. 'It could have been blowing from a hundred metres or ten kilometres away, I just couldn't tell.' The expanse of pine trees offered no perspective. 'But I thought Sonia had better go.'

Richard told his wife that she should leave quickly. It was now quite dark outside, and embers and burned leaves were falling, while the wind continued to pick up. Both Richard and Sonia were determined not to panic, not least because they did not want to frighten their daughter. Richard says: 'I took Emma out and put her in the car. She was starting to wake up and I thought she might be scared if she saw me in my overalls, so I was as gentle as possible, hoping she would go back to sleep.'

Sonia says: 'I had things prepared to put in the car for Emma and me, but nothing for Richard. We were going to a barbecue later that day so I remembered to take the salad. I thought there'd be a few embers for Richard to put out and then we'd come home. It would be a ten-minute job and then we'd be off to dinner.

'I should have realised how serious things were: it was pitch black at 2.30 in the afternoon.

'Richard told me which way to drive: he knew there were roadblocks. But as I drove away I thought, this is really odd, leaving Richard.' He had been too distracted to kiss Sonia goodbye. 'I had the headlights on and there were a lot of embers falling onto the windscreen. As I was driving away from the house the sky seemed to get lighter, but then I did a ninety-degree turn and it got darker again. That's when I started to worry a lot and thinking about the next day's newspaper headlines: *Stupid thirty-eight-weeks-pregnant woman drives into fire with toddler.*'

'The route we discussed didn't feel right, because it was getting darker. I thought that maybe I should just stop. So on the mobile I rang my friend whose house I was going to, and she said, Oh, we're still here and we're fine. They had no idea. I kept going.'

Richard watched them go, then waited out the front with a neighbour. 'We were wondering when it was going to come. The smoke looked dirty, black and brown, and burning leaves and twigs were falling now, not just embers. We were starting to hear helicopters, but I realised we were in big trouble only when I saw the heli-crane down very low.

'After a minute or two I went inside to see what Sonia had prepared and check where everything was. I picked up a rake and shovel and brought them in with me, thinking that, if the fire was outside, it would be best to have them inside in case I needed them.

'The radio and the lights were on, and I realised how dark it was outside.'

The rooms suddenly became pitch black: the power had gone off in Warragamba Avenue. Richard couldn't see a thing.

'I was getting panicky. My immediate thought was to go down to the room under the house which would be safer and less likely to catch fire quickly because it had no windows on the side of the fire. I had to know that the door was unlocked so I could run down there to be safe.

'I went downstairs and checked that the door to the room was open, and then I walked back to the front of the house. The smoke was thick and blinding, and there was an enormously strong wind. Out the front was a yellow metropolitan fire tanker.'

As Richard walked forward, the embers were raining down much harder and the wind had swelled to a roar. 'The grass on the other side of the road was burning – there wasn't much organic material to burn and I couldn't believe how fierce it was. It went up like it was covered in petrol and someone had put a match to it. There was no fire front. The whole area just went up in a second.

'The fire guys yelled out, "Let's get out of here!" They didn't know I was there. I remember the sound of their boots as they ran down the footpath.'

Richard stood transfixed for several moments. And then something happened that shocked him back into action.

'Right in front of me was a wall of dark green pine trees, twenty-five to thirty metres high. You know how shops in the old days had plastic strips across the doorway to keep flies out? And how if someone walked through, you'd see their hand first, then their knee? That's how the fire was. It came through like that but in slow motion. It popped out here, then there, until there was nothing but a roaring sheet of orange and yellow and red.

'The fire was there. Right there. In front of me.' The noise was incredible: explosions, helicopters overhead. The fire sounded like flags flapping: the noise you get when you blow on the embers in a campfire, but magnified a thousand times. I knew I had to get out of there.'

Richard ran for the room under the house and slammed the door.

'When I got there I thought, There's nothing I can do. I assumed the house was burning above me. I thought about running straight out the back door but then I realised I didn't know whether I could jump the back fence, and if I couldn't do that I would be trapped.

'I was scatty, my thoughts were all over the place. I even considered running to the garage and getting my car out quickly, but the garage door was locked from the outside.' Besides, Richard could see embers and knew that if he opened the garage door they would pour inside.

'I could see out the window: all the plants and shrubs in the garden were on fire. I opened the door a little and saw the backyard burst into flames. It was raining embers, they swirled around like very heavy rain. Then the shed caught fire. The smoke was blocking out the sun ... it was pitch black. Like night.'

Now that he was somewhere relatively safe, now he was no longer overwhelmed by the fear of the fire and thoughts that he was going to die, Richard started to recover and plan. He needed to know what was happening, so he opened the door again; though he burned his hand on the handle he could get outside and start using the hose. 'I went in and out of the room a few times, but had to keep coming back to shelter from the smoke. I was continually coughing and my eyes were watering. But each time I went outside, I could move further towards the front of the house without being overcome by the smoke or heat.

'Eventually I went right round the house and realised that, though the yard was ablaze and the shed was being destroyed, the house itself was okay.

'I saw my neighbour Greg come outside just then and asked whether he was okay. He said he was, but we were both concentrating on hosing everything we could find, so we didn't talk for long.

'I had a pile of wood on the southwestern corner about five metres from the house. Emma's paddling pool was nearby so I tipped the water over the woodpile, but the wood burst back into flames almost immediately. I hosed, and they would burn again and again.'

Richard felt that as long as he could keep the fires away from the house, it was not in any immediate danger.

'I thought the deck would catch fire, so I went up there and hosed it down and got caught in the hose, which kinked – I thought it was going to stop working. There were embers all over the deck. Some had landed on the roof, which was made of poly sheeting which they'd melted, and they had dropped through to the deck below. I was hosing anything and everything around the house, but I didn't bother with the grass or trees, which I knew would burn anyway. I was focused on fires and any embers a metre or two around the edge of the house.'

Paling fences between homes proved to be one of the prime conductors of the flames; Richard's fence caught alight and he hosed it down immediately, as the flames were quite close to the eaves.

Richard, who was now reacting clearly and purposefully, recalls thinking that the fire was doing exactly as he thought it would. 'Except it was all happening much faster and the heat and flames were magnified. If you tried to burn that fence the flames wouldn't be as high as they were. You can see why people think things explode ... an ember lands and whatever is under it catches fire like a match.'

Now things seemed to be under better control, Richard thought of his neighbours. He and Greg went to two neighbouring houses and realised that if they could get hoses onto the fires there, they might be able to save them.

'We were both concerned that embers might get into our own roofs, so one of us would stay to watch our houses and the other would go to see what was happening up the street.' They went from house to house hosing down flames and then returning to check on their own places. They saw smoke coming from under the eaves of number 75 and managed to hose it down.

Richard says: 'I met a guy who lived in a demountable in the backyard of 75, saying his place out the back had gone up and his Harley Davidson was in the garage of the house out the front. He asked us to help him with it. But the bike was locked so we had to carry it up the driveway and lift it onto a ute. He drove away, and we watched the house burn down.'

By now Richard and Greg had prevented four neighbours' houses from burning down on a street that bore the full brunt of the Canberra firestorm. Richard took a breather and called Sonia. 'I was really worried that she had no idea what had happened. I had nearly been killed, but I was okay.' He managed to call his father and get him to pass the message on.

Richard was still worried about his own house, however. 'I wasn't paying enough attention to the roof cavity. I should have stayed in the house because if any of the windows had gone in, I couldn't have done anything and the house would have been on fire; embers would have blown in and there would have been nothing I could do. Instead of hiding downstairs I should have stayed in the house and focused on the rooms most likely to be under threat.'

Terrified that embers might reach the roof, Richard patrolled his house all night. The water pressure began to diminish, so he and Greg filled buckets and cans with water just in case.

If the water supply in Warragamba Avenue had failed, as it did in so many other places during the Canberra firestorm, the outcome for the Stantons and their neighbours would have been very different. Because Richard's house was relatively free of debris around the outside, he might have been able to stamp out small fires, but if the houses up the street had continued to burn fiercely, the houses could easily have incinerated each other, one by one. That happened in many places in Canberra during this period.

Richard says: 'My eyes were killing me; I couldn't look at bright light and was constantly pouring water on my face to ease the pain. I should have used goggles and a mask, but I didn't know that. I ended up needing treatment for burned eyes.'

Fire experts came to examine the damage to Warragamba Avenue the following day. They estimated that the energy produced by the flames was around 50,000 kilowatts per metre, equivalent to 50,000 single-bar heaters per metre of forest. Mature pine trees in the reserve had been snapped like matchsticks by winds that might have reached 250 kilometres per hour.

Richard said: 'We walked up the street late on the night of the fire with a couple of policemen, one on foot, the other in a car. The guy on foot was shining his torch on each house and calling out to his mate to record the situation: Number 79 burnt to the ground, nil persons. Number 81, burnt to the ground, nil persons, number 83, burned to the ground, nil persons ... I remember thinking, How the hell does he know there's nobody in there? There was no way those people could have got out.'

In fact, four people died in the Canberra fires that day.

TWO

ONE DAY FROM THE VALLEY . . .

Jane and Rick Smyth came to Canberra in the 1970s, seeking a rural lifestyle with city amenities. They bought a one-acre block in the new suburb of Chapman south of the city, not far from the Murrumbidgee Valley and close to horse paddocks, with a nature reserve behind. They built their house on the side of a hill with wide views: from their home in Chauvel Circle they could see the Captain Cook Memorial Fountain in Lake Burley Griffin and in due course the mast and flag of the new Parliament House.

After thirty years, the Smyths lived comfortably in their brick, timber-decked house: their children had left home and they had two cars, much-loved paintings on the walls and a beautiful native garden. The whole family had always loved the Australian bush. Jane said: 'Shortly after we arrived in Canberra we went to an exhibition by the Society for Growing Australian Plants and were bowled over by the variety of colours and perfumes. So we made our own garden, because we knew that indigenous plants use less water and attract native birds. In our garden we had spotted pardalotes, kookaburras, currawongs, magpies, wrens, flame robins, native pigeons, cockatoos, sparrow hawks, owls ... Below the house was an area we called the bog, which was fed by water from higher up the hill, and where a bowerbird had built a nest.

'We had a huge eucalypt in front of the house and a couple of other gum trees, and we added hundreds of native trees and shrubs. Our three kids played in the surrounding bush. Sometimes on the weekend Rick would disappear into the garden for hours with just his radio for company, and he'd come back and say, "We are living in Paradise."'

Leaf litter built up and was home to lizards, snakes and echidnas. 'We were told it was really dangerous in case of bushfires,' said Jane, 'but it was home to the native animals and we were reluctant to destroy the habitat by clearing.'

Nevertheless, the Smyths were aware of the fire threat. In the late 1990s a fire had broken out in the other side of the hill, about 500 metres away; fortunately this burned out. The December 2001 bushfires were more serious; they burned out 500 hectares and came right to the heart of Canberra. On another occasion strong winds caused powerlines in the open space behind the houses to clash, with sparks starting a small grass fire underneath. The ACT Rural Fire Brigade quickly extinguished the flames before any private property was damaged.

2002 was a drought year with a scorching summer, and the Smyths became uneasily aware that they probably needed to plan for a fire emergency, just in case. Jane: 'I said to Rick: "One day a huge fire will come out of the valley. I hope it's not in our lifetime."' A home-based consultant and natural organiser, Jane began liaising with neighbours so they could work together to protect themselves and their properties from bushfire. They agreed to check hoses and tap fittings and to familiarise themselves with the water supply provisions in neighbouring properties.

The Rural Fire Service agreed to send two volunteers to talk to about twenty residents of Chauvel Circle about emergency measures. (The volunteers were unused to doing this, and nervously apologised for possibly spoiling new sofa covers with their working clothes.) Everybody assumed that the fires would come over the hills behind the houses, and were reassured when the volunteers told them that fire travelled fastest uphill, so they would be all right. The volunteers told them to wear clothes that covered the whole body, to protect eyes and hands with goggles, masks and gloves, and to wear wide-brimmed hats to repel ashes.

Firefighting was thirsty work, so they would need drinking water handy. The basic message was: shelter inside the house, close and seal up as much as possible, use wet towels and take the hose inside the house because it would be needed afterwards to attack the fire after the front had passed. The residents were advised to have someone inside the house to check for embers and sparks, as well as someone outside.

Jane remembers feeling reassured because the fire depot was only a few minutes away. 'We were all reasonably healthy, and we expected to be able to cope if we had to, and if we followed the guidelines carefully. They convinced us to stay at home until we were told to leave. They said we could rely on the police, who would warn us in time, and the evacuation would be conducted in a very orderly fashion.' Jane and Rick bought goggles, suitable clothes and gloves and placed them in the laundry, replaced their wooden ladder with a steel one, bought torches and cleaned out the guttering.

In early January 2003, lightning storms started hundreds of fires in the Kosciuszko and Namadgi Ranges west of Canberra. Gale force winds fanned the flames and the humidity decreased day by day. ABC Canberra Local Radio worried about bushfires for more than a week, and Rural Fire Brigade volunteers went to deal with fires deep in the national parks. Canberra residents grew increasingly anxious, but the emergency authorities remained reassuring. Some residents of Chauvel Circle left for their holidays in Melbourne, the coast or a jazz festival north of Sydney.

On Saturday 18 January, Jane was filled with a sense of foreboding. 'It was thirty-six or thirty-seven degrees, and we knew the fires in the mountains were out of control. Rick went off to the surgery in the morning' – he was a dentist – 'but I decided not to go to the markets or to a housewarming we'd been invited to that afternoon. I just thought someone should watch the house.

'I grew more and more nervous. I had a long conversation on the phone with a friend in Tasmania, then I washed, ironed and cleaned practically everything. This isn't normal behaviour for me on a Saturday, but I had to keep busy to quell my anxiety. The house was beautiful. As I cleaned I looked at our artwork and tried to work out what I would save if the house were threatened.'

Jane left her car in the carport facing the street and made sure she had the keys in her pocket. She brought their black Labrador Satchmo inside, put her wallet, jewellery and some precious family photos in her handbag and placed it on the bed.

The phone rang: it was a neighbour at the North Coast Jazz Festival who had heard about the fires threatening Canberra. 'Should we come home?' she asked.

It was a terrible question. Jane said: 'I told them things really couldn't be any worse, but we hadn't heard anything. There had been no warnings and I guessed that we would have been told if there was real danger. So I said, "I think you should come back as soon as the concert finishes ... I'll call you if anything changes."'

Jane put the phone down. She noticed that the wind had suddenly picked up, with leaves and dust flying in all directions, and that smoke had blacked out the sun. She called back the neighbour immediately and said: 'Come home. It's blowing a gale here. I've got to go.'

A warning came over the radio that residents of Chapman and Duffy were advised to return to their homes. Jane called Rick in his surgery and told him to come home as soon as he could; she also made phone calls to some neighbours and asked them to call others. She filled the bath with water, moved the furniture away from windows, closed all the doors and put on her fire clothes. While she was doing this, a small grass fire started in a reserve behind the property, which neighbours quickly extinguished.

Rick finally arrived. Jane says: 'I said, "Quick, here's your clothes, get changed." He'd been in a cool, quiet pale green dental surgery and was a bit confused. We couldn't see any fire or embers at that stage, but the wind was getting fiercer all the time and smoke was everywhere.'

Still no call to evacuate came from the emergency agencies. 'Our first priority was to saturate the house and garden as much as we could, but the air was so dry that the water just evaporated.

Embers started landing in the shrubs and setting the leaves alight. It just kept getting worse and worse: I could hear shouts coming from neighbouring properties and realised everybody was working frantically. From our front deck we could see the horse paddocks and I saw tail and brake lights through the smoke. They must have been trying to move the horses.

'We were very busy very quickly, but amazingly calm too. I'm not sure why. I suppose it was because we had a job to do and we focused on that: panicking was pointless.'

Jane and Rick gradually realised that they were on their own. 'There was no one to help us. No fire service, no police. And we knew that all our neighbours were in the same situation.

'Rick and I were coping quite well, managing to put out little fires in the garden and close to the house. We both worked really fast. I remember leaping across the pot plants in the courtyard and thinking I was quite athletic when I needed to be. I thought, This is good, I can do this, I can keep this up for a few hours, and the danger will be over.

'A helicopter came over very low. I thought I saw a cameraman inside and started to worry about our elderly parents in Sydney. I thought, Oh no, they're going to see us on a news bulletin fighting a fire ... they'll worry, and who will look after them?'

That change of thought made Jane consider the bigger picture. 'For the first time I thought, this is horrible, this is really bad.' She and Rick, however, met on the deck and reassured each other: 'We said, yes, we can save the house, this is okay.'

Then they heard a shuddering, massive roar. The line of conifers on the western edge of the Smyths' property – not from behind the house as they had expected — became a huge, travelling wall of fire.

'The flames came straight towards us,' says Jane. 'It was raining fire. Rick shouted, "Get inside!"

'I was holding the hose, which I had intended to take into the house so that afterwards we could go back outside and continue fighting the fire. But I had to drop it and run.' The hose caught alight on the deck.

Jane and Rick fled into the lounge room. 'It was looking beautiful with gorgeous summer roses in a bowl and the ceiling fan circling overhead, and ABC-FM playing gentle music in the background. And there was a roaring inferno outside. We looked at each other and asked: "What do we do now?"

'We tried to remember how long a fire front took to pass, which we thought was a couple of minutes. So we waited, but nothing seemed to be improving. It just seemed to be getting worse.'

The timber door and window frames caught alight. And then something happened that made Jane and Rick forget all their calm resolutions to follow instructions to stay inside. Jane: 'The window suddenly cracked right across, and a web of smaller cracks began to run along the glass very fast. We knew that if the windows broke and fell in, the entire interior of the house would go up. We stood calmly watching this for a moment or two, then Rick said: "I think we've got to go . . . *NOW!*"'

Rick went to grab the dog: Jane opened the side door. 'We couldn't get outside. There was a pergola that was dropping leaves or branches in balls of fire. I tried another door at the back of the house, and the fire had moved around there too.

'Then Rick remembered being told that it was safest to go where a fire had been because everything was already burned. That meant leaving by the front door. It felt as if we had to run into the fire, rather than away from it.'

While Rick struggled to pick up the dog, which was reluctant to move, Jane opened the front door and fled. 'It was very, very black. But through the black smoke there were all these sparks and flashes and little fires from the bushes and shrubs. It was actually rather beautiful. But there was nothing burning on the path. I picked my way along this black corridor and reached an area behind the house which had burned earlier.'

From her vantage point of relative safety, Jane looked around, expecting to see Rick behind her, carrying Satchmo. He wasn't there.

'I thought, He's tripped, he's fallen down the stairs, he's hurt his head, he's been overcome by smoke getting the dog out. I've got to go back down that path into the house and find him.

'Then I thought: If he's fallen, how am I going to get him out? I panicked. Then I remembered those brave people in the Bali fire and said to myself, I just have to do this.'

Jane took a huge breath and retraced her steps. She still couldn't see Rick, and was nearly at the house when she saw a dark figure. She called, 'Who's that?'

'Who the bloody hell do you think it is?' shouted Rick.

Jane and Rick, who was carrying Satchmo swathed in wet towels, walked quickly back to the area down the slope and behind the house. Jane says: 'It was still pretty wild with the fierce wind and embers everywhere. We lay on our stomachs, put our hands over our heads, told the dog to stay down and covered him with a wet towel.'

With Satchmo, Jane and Rick lay there in the smoke while the fire roared around them. They did not touch each other but Jane felt the relief of just being together. After about ten minutes they thought the noise was receding and felt safe enough to sit up.

'Because we were sitting on the slope, we were in the front stalls for the whole unfolding disaster,' says Jane. 'We sat there and watched the whole neighbourhood burn.' They could see houses were beginning to catch fire around them. 'Some of our neighbours' houses were burning quite quickly. Some stayed untouched for a while, then we'd see smoke coming out from gutters, then the roofs, and then there would be a great crash. We saw this lovely blue flame as people's gas heaters caught alight.

'And in front of us, our house was burning to the ground.

'It was torture,' says Jane, her voice a little unsteady. 'We had to leave so quickly when we were in danger, and yet the house was catching fire so slowly. I knew my handbag was still on my bed, and that part of the house wasn't alight yet. But we couldn't go inside because we didn't know when the roof would fall in, or something would explode.

'Then the house was fully alight; we could see the orange flames in different rooms.

'Rick felt as helpless as I did. He asked, "Isn't there something I can do? Should I go back inside?" And I told him, "If you go back in there, it's all over between us."'

They laughed, taking refuge in black humour. 'We sat up there saying, "How many fire trucks would it take to save our house?" I said six and Rick said five, and we laughed because we hadn't heard a single siren. No police, no firefighters, nothing. Busy somewhere else, we said.'

They sat in the ashes a little longer, watching the light show. Gradually the house fires died down and people began to reappear. A neighbour to the east of the Smyths came through the smoke with a tray of cool drinks and some salmon sandwiches. 'We hugged and she consoled us. And we sat there eating those delicious sandwiches and saying, "Smoked salmon, not bad is it?"'

Afterwards, Jane, Rick and Satchmo walked along their street, surveying the devastation. They came across a woman who was almost hysterical because she had left her animals at home and when she returned there was nothing left. The Smyths comforted her: they could have done with some comfort of their own.

Jane says, 'At the time we did not understand the scale of the disaster. A neighbour said she thought there must be about a hundred houses gone.'

In fact, 480 houses were destroyed in Chapman and Duffy that Saturday.

THREE

DON'T PANIC

Ric Hingee comes from a family of high achievers. He was born in 1943 in Canberra where his father Hin Gee Chung, a civil and structural engineer, was among the early settlers who came to design and build the new national capital. (The locals called him Bill Hingee, and the surname stuck.) Ric became an investment analyst after working for the government for some years; his equable temperament serve him well in handling the volatile share market. 'I am not the type who panics,' he says. 'In fact, I am very much against any form of panic; I don't believe anyone can think properly if they're panicking. As long as I'm confident in the decisions I'm making, I am quite relaxed.'

A methodical, organised man, Ric, his English-born wife

Melissa and their children settled in Duffy on the urban fringe of Canberra. 'Living there means I can get off into the countryside,' explains Ric. 'The river is nearby so I go swimming and kayaking. I like to be able to look back over Canberra; I can see the lake and the fountain, and the direction of the spray tells me whether I can go windsurfing or sailing. Very handy.

'I've always been interested in sports, especially those that are dangerous but where you take calculated risks. I like avalanche skiing and whitewater kayaking, even caving; they're not for everybody, I know, but I enjoy them because I like testing myself under stress, having my adrenalin levels pushed along.'

The Hingees settled in Eildon Place, a street often mentioned in local media as one of the best in Canberra for community spirit. This made it attractive to Ric and Melissa. 'I believe in fairness, people helping each other,' says Ric. 'I don't like people who refuse to take responsibility or be accountable for their actions.'

'We had very good relationships with the neighbours,' adds Melissa. 'So good we had no fences: we had to get council permission *not* to build them.'

Ric had a hand in designing and building his house, one street back from the edge of Duffy on the eastern slopes of a small hill. Windows on one side looked over the suburbs of Canberra, all the way to Parliament House and Black Mountain, while at the front houses rose up on the other side of the street. A pine plantation covered the hills behind these houses.

'Ours was a low-line timber house, built on a sloping block,' says Ric. 'It started off as eighteen and a half squares, but I doubled the size. We used a lot of timber in it: western red cedar and Oregon, and a lot of cedar panelling and shelving, and the eaves were wooden too.

'I loved the house and its surroundings. We started a garden with fishponds, fountains, and a rainforest area. One of our neighbours was a research forester and his wife ran a nursery, so we developed our native gardens together. We had many trees: spotted gums, Tasmanian blue gums, melaleucas, acacias, stringybarks, snow gums. Some had trunks almost a metre in circumference. The ground covers were also natives, although Melissa and I also introduced many exotic European-style trees and flowers.

'The trees would have been within a metre of the house. If you looked out, it was a garden full of native birds. It was fantastic, people loved it. We had an aerial photo taken, showing four houses all landscaped together, looking like an oasis.

'It was a haven for kids,' says Melissa. 'The sort of garden they love to play in. We had rabbits, a hamster, a lot of chickens and fish. Christopher spent most of his childhood outside.'

However, conscious that what was beautiful could also be a firetrap, the Hingees had begun thinning out their vegetation and taking out trees. 'I made a point of knowing about fires,' says Ric. 'I even did a bit of training as a firefighter.' His awareness, like that of his neighbours, was heightened during the Yarralumla bushfires of 2001.

'We always felt that if there was going to be danger we would be informed,' he says. 'During the Yarralumla fires we had police driving around with megaphones and plenty of warnings. So we did what we could about the house, we thought. We watered it down, and hosed the garden, but we agreed that if fire got into the garden there was nothing we could do. The houses around us were very much like ours: timber houses completely surrounded by large trees and bush gardens. All we could do, we thought, was to get out quickly when we had to, taking our important things with us. The key things were photographs: I had photos going back to my childhood and I used to be a freelance photographer, so we had photos and film of the birth of the kids, and film of every stage of their lives. We also had books, jewellery, furniture and paintings and Melissa's artworks.'

Ric and Melissa were prepared to evacuate if necessary, but they were not required to do so. 'But after 2001 we changed our attitude towards fire,' says Ric. 'I thinned out trees and chopped down the ones close to the house. I cleared a lot of ground cover and vegetation, cleared the roof regularly and had hoses on various taps around the house. We figured we'd fight a fire until we couldn't do any more, then we'd clear out.'

In January 2003, Ric was not worried at first. The fires appeared to be more or less contained in the national parks, not moving any closer to Canberra. On the morning of Saturday 18th Ric and his neighbour went to work as usual; Melissa and their son Christopher were out.

Ric worked in his Yarralumla office doing some economic analysis, but after several hours he began to feel uneasy.

'I could hear the wind picking up,' he says. 'It grew stronger and stronger. I stopped working and went out and could see billowing smoke, which I hadn't noticed before. In the distance I could see light, but I wasn't sure whether it came from flames or sparks. I thought it didn't look too good, but I had heard no warnings over the radio or TV.'

Still anxious, Ric closed up the office and drove home, arriving in the early afternoon.

'By the time I got home there was burning material falling out of the sky. The neighbours weren't around, but they had started my sprinkler system. I put my safety gear on, locked up the dog, and put some boxes out ready to put in the car if I had to go in a hurry.'

Ric was alone in the street. He had no idea what was about to happen, but the ember shower was clearly serious, and he started hosing down little spot fires. The phone rang, interrupting his work. It was Ric's brother, who said he had heard that parts of Canberra were on fire and wanted to know if he was all right. 'I realised what was about to happen and said, "No, I'm not, I might soon be on fire," and I hung up.'

Almost immediately the radio went off and Ric realised that the power had been cut. He was now quite isolated. Picking up the hose, he went outside to see what could be done.

'Leaves, embers and flames, quite a lot of dead stuff as well, was pattering down all over the place. The amount of falling debris was increasing by the minute. At first it would burn out when it hit the ground, then the pieces got larger and the wind got stronger.

'I don't remember being afraid at that stage. Then the tree out the back of the house burst into flames. It wasn't a very big tree, but there was a great deal of fire. And all the little fires on the ground started to burn, rather than being blown out by the wind. I looked around and saw that many other trees were on fire too, although not on my property. The deck on a house up the hill was on fire.

'Neighbours packed everything into their car and took off without saying anything.' People who had shared each other's lives for years went, without staying to help each other.

'At this point it was everyone for themselves,' says Ric. 'I think everyone could see that nobody would be silly enough to stay on.'

Ric was still outside using the hose but water pressure was failing. 'Everything was black, really hot, really noisy, really windy, and there was the added noise of helicopters. They were dumping water on the forests and I thought, Why aren't they dumping it on the houses? The wind and the noise and the flames were unbelievable. It was a real towering inferno. I was thinking, It can't get any worse than this.'

Then, oddly enough, it grew better. The wind dropped, the sun came out and the noise decreased. It was fine and sunny but with embers and twigs falling out of the sky still. 'I couldn't work it out,' says Ric. 'There was no reason for the fire to suddenly stop. Then about five minutes later, the wind and embers and smoke came back, all at once. The fire got worse; now my trees started to catch alight. I looked behind me and saw that all the other houses in the immediate area, and all the trees, were burning.

'That's when I said to myself, I am going to have to start thinking about getting out of here. But I still had some water, so I kept on fighting. I was annoyed that they said you could stay and fight these fires, and stamp out the little fires after the front had gone past. There was no way you could stamp out those fires: there were just too many of them.'

Then the water supply failed completely.

'That's when I decided there was no point in staying any longer. It was too hot to bear. I really thought my clothes would spontaneously combust. I was having trouble breathing, and I could feel the heat of the air through the mask I was wearing. The roar drowned out all sound: it was like thunder. I couldn't hear cars, or helicopters, or even the fire crackling.

'The flames were bright and white and yellow, not so much red. It was very hard to see. The flames didn't cast light on the trees and houses around them: the light seemed to be absorbed by the smoke.'

Ric looked up to the top of the hill. Between the houses he could see the edge of the pine forest that ran along the western edge of Canberra. 'The fireballs were blowing into the sky where the forest stopped. The flames were burning beyond the trees. I couldn't work out what was going on; I expected a well-defined fire front, but these flames were disconnected. Every now and again they would break away, and there would be a clear gap between the main fire and these flares, which seemed to be suspended in the sky. The flares were different shapes, mostly like elongated footballs or a cloud.'

Though he was ready to leave, Ric remembered that he hadn't seen the neighbour behind his house. 'I thought, I can't leave without checking. She was a close friend, and I had to go and look for her.' In the pitch black he ran down the driveway to the neighbour's house. There was no car in the driveway.

'I decided she must have gone after all, so I turned around and started running back towards my house at half pace. It was so dark I could hardly see where I was going. I thought: If you panic you get into trouble. If you build into your consciousness that you are not to panic, and you are to be relatively careful, it comes naturally. I was thinking: Next step, get the dog.

'The flames detached from the main fire and were moving down the drive like water down a river gully. They seemed to funnel down, totally independent of the main fire. I thought: These things could explode and there'll be fireballs erupting all around me. For the first time I worried about my own safety.'

Ric began racing towards the house. And the flames caught him, scorching his back and burning holes in his shirt. 'I came very close to being seriously injured; I'd left it too long to leave. And I knew I wasn't in control, I thought if this one could get me, there would be others.'

Ric made it into the house, which was not yet on fire. He grabbed the dog, which refused to move. 'So I had to pick her up bodily and take her out to the car and throw her into the back seat. I looked back.

'The house still wasn't alight, but the house next door was. I thought, I have to go back inside and get some things. I knew I could get in and out quickly.' Ric grabbed photograph albums and everything on the sideboard, piled it all into boxes, hurled them into the car and took off.

'I saw nobody in the street. Not a soul. No one walking, nobody running, no cars. But when I got round the corner there was a traffic jam near the service station. I drove up onto the nature strip, heading for the middle of the nearby sports ground. I drove to where I thought the middle of the oval was but got out and found I was nowhere near the middle, that's how little light there was. The service station blew up, gas bottles, everything. There were flames everywhere. I got back into the car and drove away again.'

Ric drove to his office, where he found Melissa and Christopher. Roadblocks had prevented them from getting home.

Melissa says: 'He appeared and I was so relieved. But he didn't behave the way I expected. He was like a charged particle of electricity, and he kept saying: "I have to go back, I've got to go back." None of this, "Honey I'm so glad you're all right." I was a bit peeved about that."

Ric's office became a makeshift evacuation centre. 'We stayed there that night,' says Melissa. 'Chris was very stressed. It was familiar surroundings, but there was one slight snag: it was a timber building with shingles, and it was raining cinders. Later that night as we were trying to sleep Chris was crying because he thought the house we were in would burn down.'

Melissa and Ric returned to their property the next day. They discovered that dozens of houses in their neighbourhood had been destroyed, including their own. 'There was nothing left,' says Melissa. 'The chickens and fish got roasted. We never saw the fish again, not even their skeletons. The neighbours across the road tied their dog up so they knew where it was, but they took off in such a hurry they forgot it, and the dog died.'

Ric and Melissa rebuilt their home on the block, taking special care to make it a fire-safe fortress. Sixteen out of twenty-four houses in Eildon Place were destroyed. But more than property went in the 2003 fires: the community spirit went too. Those whose homes were untouched felt guilty, or were angry that neighbours were able to build new homes with insurance money. Friendships were severed, relationships fractured. In Eildon Place there are no more street parties.

FOUR

THE VOLUNTEER

Volunteer fire captain Val Jeffery knows about fire. He was knee-high to a grasshopper when he saw the 1939 fires around Canberra; he was caught in a fearsome burn-over when a wind change caused a fire to engulf his 760-hectare property in 1979. And because he knew what could happen, and because in January 2003 he saw fires burning in the Brindabellas, he wrote to the farmers of the towns and villages around Tharwa, near Canberra, on 14th, wanting to give them time to prepare. His words were:

FIRE SITUATION UPDATE AND WARNING

Out-of-control fires are burning in the ranges west of us. These fires stretch from Weejasper to the north of us through to the Victorian border. Even if these fires are brought under control before the inevitable windy west to northwest change arrives, it will be almost impossible to hold them within containment lines. The only thing that can prevent this occurrence is good rain. I must say that there is no indication that this rainfall may arrive.

In short, I am writing to warn you that there is a very real possibility that these fires will break out of the mountains. At this stage it is looking like this could happen about Monday or Tuesday ... When these fires break out of the mountains they will burn virtually all our country. Suppression forces will be overwhelmed, so you will need to ensure that you are well prepared to protect your own property, and this can be very successful with a few simple precautions and preparation.

The rest of the note explains the preparations people might make.

There is a lot to be learned from a bloke like Val. Country towns throughout Australia often have a resident like him, who will irritate the bureaucrats because they don't always follow the 'guidelines' and become frustrated by occupational health and safety rules. These are the men and women who repeatedly tell inquiries and inquests that 'you ignore local knowledge at your peril' and who plead for bigger firebreaks and fuel-reduction programs. They sometimes fall foul of environmentalists who want to end cattle grazing and forest clearing to protect native flora and fauna, but essentially Val and his ilk are practical people whose most important role, as they see it, is the protection of lives and homes.

Val's town is Tharwa, on the Murrumbidgee River about fifteen kilometres south of Canberra. It has about a dozen houses, a primary school and a ramshackle general store. Around the town are another dozen or so homes, as well as the Outward Bound school. The area is mixed farming country with an emphasis on merinos and the relatively new industry of tourism: people come from the cities to enjoy the serenity, the open pastures, laconic people, and landscape.

Tharwa is overlooked by Mt Tennant and surrounded by low-forested hills to the south and west. The Murrumbidgee runs through it, but at Tharwa it is only a trickle, and sometimes it dries up altogether. After a long drought Tharwa is a bushfire haven; somewhere nearby every year fires break out. Mostly they are contained in a paddock or a shed, and most of the volunteers' work consists of reducing fuel along roads and around the town.

Val's been attending fires in Tharwa since he was old enough to do what he was told. He calculates he has been to 600 or 700. He's the founder of the ACT Volunteer Bushfire Brigade Association, has been Chairman of the ACT Bushfire Council and won an Australian Fire Service medal. He's well past retirement age now, but he is still shepherding his group of volunteers to protect Tharwa and the outlying farms as best they can.

'We've got the biggest volunteer fire brigade in the ACT,' says Val with pride. There are about one hundred on the list, and about forty active members. The fire brigade has two tankers and two light units, as well as a four-wheel-drive vehicle for the captain. Some years ago money was raised in the community to enable Val to distribute radios and now, when the Bushfire Brigade frequencies are jammed – as they often are – people can still talk to each other locally.

The natural gathering place for everyone in town is the post office and general store: it's the brigade headquarters during fires. Val's father built it and Val took it over when he was only fourteen, as well as running the family farms and transport business. It's a somewhat ramshackle affair made of cream weatherboard with a fraying corrugated-iron roof. But, like so many of these general stores, it seems to stock everything: antiques and collectables, strong liquor, canisters from the turn of the century stocking a range of goods: sago, starch, salt, oatmeal, split peas, biscuits, Bushells and Yoga teas. There is also a supply of Bon Ami, Mobil oil, Scissors cigarettes and 'pure coffee'. It's not easy to find what you want, but it's okay to ask: this isn't Coles or Woolworths.

Val Jeffery likes people and sees good in everyone, but he doesn't suffer fools gladly and he expects people to take responsibility for themselves and their circumstances. He's wily about the ways of the world, mixing as easily with grubby kids rounding up lizards as with smart government suits.

He talks about fire with respect and a great deal of knowledge, but not fear. He doesn't describe the size of the flames, or the colours, or the atmosphere; to him, fires are all pretty straightforward. 'It's not the big head-on fight with a fire you've got to be afraid of,' he says. 'If you get into a head-on fight, it's too late: stand back and let it go because you can't do a bloody thing about it. You've got to stop it getting established and that's the little stuff. Every fire starts small. If you can get to it when it's small, you should be able to stop houses burning down in most circumstances.'

Val strongly believes that people should be home to defend their properties. But who should stay and defend a town?

'Kids under ten should leave, but older than that – oh, maybe from about thirteen – they're OK. It's important to teach kids about fires. That's why country kids have an advantage over city kids. Older people, well, that depends on their health. Up to sixty I wouldn't call them old and I'd like to think you wouldn't say they were old at seventy either! By that time, they've got common sense and maturity. Sure they aren't as active as they were, but they don't have to be.

'Tourists – they're a pain in the butt, like sightseers. You've got to get them to buggery out of the place in case of fire. You'll get the one-off good one, I've found them over the years and once I picked a bloke up on the side of the road and he was a big help, but don't depend on it. These people aren't in tune with fire and the bush.'

Val's advice to newcomers is straightforward: 'Clear up around the property. Too many trees around the house are no good if you want to save the house in bushfire.' The town is on tank water, and the fire brigade can pump water from a hole near town. 'We have to make sure people don't use too much water,' he says. 'We don't encourage people to spray roofs and gardens; you use too much that way, and we can't afford it out here.'

Early in January 2003, Val and his small teams were called on to help contain the fires up in the Brindabellas. He thinks some of them could have been put out if more people were called upon, but they weren't, and the bushfires moved relentlessly east and south. 'This is when I pulled my belt in a few notches,' said Val laconically. He started warning people about the fires, encouraging them to prepare their properties and stay in town. 'The fires would come to Tharwa, anyone could see that,' he says.

He distributed his now-famous warning to residents:

- Ensure your buildings are well clear of flammable materials.
- Be prepared to stay at home on the expected bad fire days.
- Do not evacuate unless you are scared or invalided. If you do leave, leave well ahead of the fire.

- If you have a few able-bodied friends who can be with you, invite them along.
- Make sure you have any weed spray units or pumps etc., set up and filled with water ready to go.
- Do not rely on electric pressure pumps as you can expect to lose power.
- Keep filled buckets around your buildings, complete with a mop if possible.
- Muster stock into bare paddocks or yards well ahead of the fire.

DON'T PANIC. This is not the Blue Mountains, and with a bit of common sense everyone should be safe and no property should be lost.

I don't want to alarm people, just to forewarn you.

All the best and keep safe.

Cheers

Val Jeffery

PS For Tharwa residents

Our water supply is deteriorating rapidly but I am still able to pump, but for how long I don't know. Please do not waste any water. When we get fires coming into the village or nearby, please ensure that NO hoses are running. If a fire comes over the village, be very conservative with usage, do not hose buildings or

gardens down for the sake of it. Use common sense.
I could use some assistance over the weekend to do
some digging in the river. An early morning wander
round the village found hoses that had obviously been
on all night. DO THE RIGHT THING.

   Val 14/1/03

Val and his volunteers did some backburning around the edge of Tharwa, and would like to have done more. By now the fires had been in the hills for more than two weeks, burning along ridge tops and smoking out the towns on days when the wind blew from the northwest.

Val expected the fires to arrive on Monday 20th or Tuesday 21st. But on Saturday morning he received word that the fire was starting to run. 'We were getting spot fires around the area,' he says. 'The fire built up in intensity, we got a lot of smoke.

'The embers were from the back of Mt Tennant about four or five kilometres away. Most spot fires came from the back of the hills, not the front; the eddies develop down the back of the hills. It's a mistake to wait till you can see flames on the side of the hill facing you.

'I knew we were in trouble, but I wasn't expecting the fire to hit quite as savagely as it did. With only two tankers and three light units for the whole area from Paddy's River south through Tharwa to Naas, we were, to put it mildly, stretched.

'Calls were coming in for assistance, especially from the Naas area which was hit first. We had one fire truck and a light unit in town, and I tried to get through with the one tanker and one light unit I had available, but we were halted by the sheer ferocity of the firestorm that came down from the mountain. We were bloody lucky we hadn't been a few minutes earlier or we would have been caught right in the middle of it and all incinerated. We retreated and tried to get round the other way.

'With the fire truck and light unit in town, we tried to get through to the south, where we were getting reports of houses in real danger. But the fire had come down over the road and it was just impossible to get through. A house burned down on the outskirts of Tharwa, and we weren't there to help.

'By this time the fire was roaring down Spring Station Creek, which is between Tharwa and where we were getting the spot fires. The creek acted as a wick and drew the fire down to the south of the town. We started to get pressure on the Outward Bound school then, so we took a truck up there to see what we could do.

'On the way we came across a cottage that looked like it was having big problems. I'd been happy for the owner to leave: she was a retired lady who had cleaned everything out and gone to her daughter's place in Canberra. But there was a big pine tree on the western side of the house, and as we drove up the fire hit it. It went right over the house. I thought it was gone. But then the fire suddenly dropped out of the tree because there wasn't enough fuel left. It started spot fires on the lawn, so we drove in. She'd left a hose connected, which was good, because she had plenty of water. So even without the tanker I was able to put the spot fires out, and that house was saved.

'We went up to the Outward Bound school to see if they needed help, putting out a few spot fires along the road. A trailer full of rubbish was alight: they'd cleaned up, but didn't move the trailer. They'd had a massive cleanup, and then these young people came into the village; they cleaned up all around so the place was in a good state. That meant that, when the fire hit, we'd have 200 feet jumping on spot fires.

'There were no major problems at the school, so we came back to the village. That's when I found a task force from the New South Wales Rural Fire Service, having a barbecue in front of the school! I tried to get them to disperse around the district, but they refused. They wouldn't do any work for me … I was really disappointed about that.

'About the same time I came across two police constables who were setting out to evacuate the village, with instructions from high up, of course. This gave me an awful shock: if we had evacuated the village we would have lost it, simple as that. You only need one spot fire that nobody tackles and the whole village goes up.

'I told the constable all this and then said, "I'll take responsibility. I'm the captain here." I said, "I know the people here." I give them credit for a bit of common sense and I think any other village in this situation would have reacted very much the same way.'

The police left. Val resumed patrolling. By now the atmosphere was black with smoke and embers. Eyes were scorched, everybody was running on adrenalin. Val calmly continued talking to people, putting out spot fires, reassuring.

'We had two nights in Tharwa that day,' he says. 'The wind was so strong you couldn't get out of the doors on one side of the vehicle. And then we started hearing things on the radio.'

Fires had now reached Canberra and were burning homes at the rate of 200 an hour. Tharwa could not expect any help.

'People in the town had to walk around and jump on fires, and they fizzled out then. Everybody was looking after everybody else. There was a lot of movement in town. I didn't need to spend a lot of time there; I knew the people there could look after the place. They had water. Some firefighters I didn't have on units were wandering around with knapsacks. Bloody handy.'

After the firestorm passed from Mt Tennant, Val was able to get through with the tanker to help in property protection at farms outside Tharwa. They could not always get through due to burn-overs, and Val was worried because he knew so many properties were on their own. 'Two houses were lost in our area, but the main firestorm passed with no lives lost and no accidents.' Val says this with quiet pride.

The wind dropped, and Val and his teams were hoping for respite. But they were in for another shock. 'We were taking advantage of the lull to secure the northern side of the village,' says Val. 'And without any warning a southerly buster hit. It whipped the fire down the unstocked Murrumbidgee corridor and linked up with a similar fire running across the Tidbinbilla Road on the northwestern edge of the village. We had to get some trucks out to deal with that.

'Fortunately in town things died down. Only two or three people left in town would have put the remaining spot fires out. But out of town one of our trucks was confronting a blaze. Head on. They did a great job in helping to save the farmer's property.'

The trucks came back into town later, saw that everything was under control, and the tired volunteers had a drink and something to eat. 'They were tired to begin with,' says Val, 'they'd had wins and disappointments and they'd saved the town.' After a short break, the trucks headed off to the east, where fires were still threatening properties.

'I got to bed very late on Saturday night. Before daylight I was woken by a phone call from Phil Blaydon, one of my deputies, to say that poplars were alight at the bottom of town and were throwing sparks into the unburnt areas in the village. So we had to get down there and deal with that.

'On the Sunday morning I had a phone call from head office telling me graders were coming to put a line right around the fire edge. I wasn't at all happy with that, and told them so: a line like that would do a lot of damage to people's property. The fire had had its go, run out of steam and wouldn't pose any threat until the next bad weather change. I told head office we didn't need the graders, but we thought they'd come in handy on the next bad fire day.

'The week after the main run there were a lot of tiring days. We hadn't any phones, which gave me a bit of peace, but it would have been hard on friends and relatives who were away from the village and who might have been worried. And the town had no power for a week. People turned up with generators to keep the base radio station working and the shop fridges working. The beer had to be kept cold, right?'

FIVE

GOOD FARMING

Every summer sees big fires around the Namadgi Ranges in the ACT. They are usually caused by lightning strikes and if they grow too big they are unstoppable. When they get away and join up, they roll over everything in their path until they run out of fuel, or it rains. People living inland know that these kinds of fires often won't stop until they get to the big firebreak: the ocean.

Farmers in these isolated properties know that they cannot expect help from fire brigades or water bombers. They know it is their responsibility to reduce the fuel load, keep their stock and homes safe, maintain their own water supply and make sure there are enough good people around to help them deal with emergencies if necessary.

John and Anna Hyles of Booroomba, a 4500-hectare grazing property in the Namadgi Ranges, knew the drill. They had heard about the big fires in the area in 1939, where property burned on a seventy-two-kilometre front, destroying 62,000 hectares of forest and killing six people. But John, who was chairman and an active member of the Tharwa Fire Brigade, felt instinctively that the next fire could be even worse.

At the end of 2002, he thought he had a rough idea what to expect. Everything pointed to disaster: drought, grazing licences suspended in the high country and in national parks, fuel loads building up, fewer backburns and firefighting efforts diminished by people leaving rural properties.

Booroomba, where Anna and John live with their three young children Charlie, William and Miranda, is a beautiful property. The homestead is at the end of a gravel road, on a small rise, with the Ranges rising behind. The track winds across open treeless country first, where the grasses feed sheep and native animals. A stand of poplars comes into view first and then other European trees are visible, sheltering the homestead and the main houses. There is a big dam out the front of the house with a small jetty, and acres of grass stretch between the dam and the homestead. A small hill comically named Big Back dominates the backyard at Booroomba. Behind it the Namadgi Ranges shade into the Brindabellas, the Snowy Mountains and the Kosciuszko Ranges.

This is a country of black snow gums, some with trunks

at ground level a metre or more across. Higher up the hills are red and yellow box, mountain ash and broad-leafed peppermint, all imposing. Up at the snowline there are more familiar grey and white-limbed snow gums, hardy small-leaved shrubs and moss.

Out the back of the homestead is a stone cottage, among the first buildings on the site, and next to that is a whitewashed weatherboard storage hut built about the turn of the century, as well as a slab-sided hut, leaning a little as timber structures do in the bush.

About 250 metres south of the homestead, on a small rise overlooking the property, is Blytheburn, another historic stone cottage built in 1882 but now unoccupied. To the north is Braeside, another rammed-earth home.

Both Booroomba and Blytheburn are important historic pioneering properties. Both were built by Charles and Elizabeth McKeahnie, Booroomba in the early 1860s, Blytheburn in 1882, as dairy and cattle properties. There is local speculation that Elizabeth McKeahnie's brother Charlie was the rider immortalised in A.B. Paterson's immortal poem 'The Man from Snowy River'. The properties passed through several hands before media baron Sir Keith Murdoch bought Booroomba in the 1940s. He loved the property, which he worked for many years with his manager, Barry Henry. John Hyles senior bought the property from Sir Keith's widow, Lady Elisabeth Murdoch, after Sir Keith's death: she thought the region too cold for her or her family. It became a superfine merino wool property, running 18,000 sheep, 600 cows and horses.

January 2003 was hot and dry, day after day. There were spot fires in the ranges, building in intensity, joining together. While they were still deep within the national parks they posed no great threat to the Hyles's properties. But John Hyles began planning to confront them.

In early January he cut a bulldozer track between the hills to give the animals a means of escape if the fires burned to the foothills. He also built and filled a million-litre dam so there was plenty of water for firefighting. Then his thoughts shifted to the homestead. At Booromba most of the sheep were mustered into the paddocks near the house where they would eat the grass to dirt. In the eighty hectares around the buildings, there was nothing left to burn; the stock was left in the paddocks.

John allowed the dams to fill from nearby springs. He bulldozed out a larger slice of the embankment of the dam near the main house and nearly doubled its size to about thirteen million litres of water. He brought water tankers in and stationed them alongside the main buildings. Hoses and pumps were attached at both ends of the tanks, able to reach around the buildings and onto the roof. Most of the fittings were of metal, though some were plastic. John and his staff cleaned around the buildings under the trees, though they did not remove the mulch and compost.

Good farming

As the fires drew nearer, John called on family, friends and staff to prepare. Some who felt they had a right to help in defending the property were disappointed not to be asked to stay. But John wanted calm, experienced and dependable people who would be reliable in a crisis. He created six teams: four would defend houses, two would be in charge of the farm firefighting units, utilities with water tanks.

Anna decided she would stay, though she had never fought a bushfire before (and secretly thought John was exaggerating the threat somewhat). Family members came to help: John's brother Alex was an experienced firefighter, and his sister Georgina and her husband Matthew came up from Sydney.

It was decided that the outbuildings and sheds would not be defended, but that the firefighters would try to save the historic homes, the storerooms, the slab-sided hut and the main houses. Other buildings were too far from sources of water.

Preparations went on for weeks and by the middle of the month Anna was rather tired of it all. The uncertainty was exhausting. Every day she would watch and listen to the news, talk to other locals, think of further preparations to be made. She tried not to frighten the children or appear obsessed. She was careful with her words. She heard about the neighbours' plans, searched for smoke or the smell of burning eucalypt.

John and Anna decided to go down to the coast for a few days for a rest: the fires were still thirty kilometres away. 'That's advice from my father, who always said you must be well rested for a big campaign,' said John. 'He learned that during the Second World War, in Greece and on Crete.' Refreshed, they returned to find that the fires were now twenty kilometres from them.

The preparations continued. The children were sent to a friend's property, well away from the scene of danger. Drums and large buckets of water were placed around all the buildings; generators and pumps were checked and the staff issued with hand-held radios. Machinery in the sheds and a paddock bomb were moved into the middle of the grass-free paddocks, the gun locker opened and the rifles and ammunition moved. Gates in the paddocks were left open to let the stock escape; John had seen sheep and cattle piled up and burned to death on a fence they were unable to get through.

Everybody had overalls, gloves, smoke masks, sunglasses and bush hats. They had formed an escape plan: take a vehicle down the track towards the main road, out through the gates near the poplars. Though they had been told the smoke would be too thick for visibility, they thought the road was wide enough to avoid fallen trees or other cars.

Saturday 18 January dawned: yet another day with temperatures in the high thirties, strong northwesterly winds and low humidity. John was sure that they would face the fires that day. His mother Pam had arrived, ready to make sandwiches and drinks for helpers. All those defending the property worked all morning, pouring as much water as possible on lawns, around trees and buildings and on verandas. There was no shortage of water, provided the fire didn't last too long and the pumps and hoses kept working.

John called them together for a meeting: 'Stick to the plan,' he told them. 'Don't leave your home to help at another because there will be a continuing threat. Two teams in light farm units will be patrolling; they'll come to you. Keep drinking fluids. Don't be heroic. We are well prepared. Thank you for staying and helping us through this.'

It grew hotter and hotter, and smoke clouds appeared over Big Back. The wind picked up, embers began falling on the nearby hills. Fires broke out sporadically along the access track to the main road, then into the grasslands. Grass around the homestead caught alight, but was quickly extinguished.

A NSW Rural Fire Service unit arrived, to everybody's gratitude: another tanker with experienced hands would be useful. However, they stayed only long enough to fill their tank with water, telling the staff that the coming firestorm was too big to face and that anyone with any sense should leave. One member of John's team thought this was good advice, and drove out behind the retreating fire truck. However, confronted by flames and smoke on the road out, he returned to his position.

The wind picked up again: smoke billowed from behind the hills and nobody knew where the firefront was. The gardens, walls and buildings were being hosed down. Motor vehicles were turned around to face the direction of the escape route and engines turned on; John had read somewhere that if seeking shelter in a vehicle during a fire the air should be switched on recirculate, as it would be cooler than the air outside. In all the homes wet towels were placed under the doors to keep out smoke and ash. The dogs were let off the chains; about eighty merino rams were placed in the shearing shed, but the horses were led to the paddocks to run free.

Anna, standing on the veranda at Blytheburn with John, watched the smoke cloud grow bigger and bigger. One moment it was just over the horizon, the next towering into the sky overhead; first it was white, then black. Anna couldn't keep her eyes off it. She filmed it on the video camera. The smoke drifted across the sun and the sky turned grey and then pink. The smell of burning bush was everywhere, the smoke scorching noses and throats. There was a rumble behind the hills like an approaching thunderstorm. Already the defenders had discovered that the sunglasses were next to useless. They failed to keep smoke out of people's eyes, and when the light drained out of the sky it was impossible to see. The sunglasses were abandoned. A massive smoke cloud doused the whole property with choking black, the wind roared. Anna turned the video camera off.

John was feeling reasonably confident. 'I thought all the scrub would burn, not the houses,' he said. 'There would be stock losses, but everything else would be okay.'

The wind rose to near gale force, the only indication, still, that the firefront was coming. The ember shower grew thicker, almost horizontal. Wherever the embers landed something caught alight: the decking, fences, sheds, mulch. Fires were breaking out everywhere, and people had to shout to be heard above the roar. There was another blast of hot wind, and day turned to night. John and Anna could not even see the watches on their wrists. The world was a maelstrom of flaring red embers, occasionally a flare as a bigger fire tore through the darkness. John and Anna couldn't see the buildings a hundred metres away.

John was watering the garden when he heard a roar like four jumbo jets taking off. Peering into the darkness, he was confronted by the most terrifying sight of his life. The air ignited, the whole sky turned a deep violent, emergency red. Booroomba was engulfed in liquid hellfire.

John says: 'I thought I was drowning in an ocean of fire. The air had caught fire. All I could think was, everybody's just been killed.'

He had enough presence of mind to run into Blytheburn and gather his thoughts. 'I thought: Well, that's it. I felt my legs getting very hot and thought I was burning. The water I'd just sprayed on my legs was scalding: the radiant heat had made it boil.

'Then I thought what I saw was a vision. Roger, one of the helpers, arrived with the low loader with the grader on it. He unloaded it and immediately the paint, lights, mirrors and tyres were all cooked. Then he left. It was unbelievable.'

Anna had also bolted inside. She rushed to the phone and called the Tharwa Rural Fire Brigade. 'I thought: Oh my God, I'm a mother with three children, I'm about to be killed,' she says.

The man on the other end of the line remained calm, and his lack of panic steadied Anna. 'I thought, I'm still alive, John is alive, Blytheburn is still standing. Matthew [a neighbour] is with us. We're all still alive.'

Anna, John and Matthew decided to get into one of the waiting cars; if the idea about recirculating air worked, they would be able to breathe if the firestorm returned. They raced to Booroomba to see whether anyone was alive, knowing what a risky thing they were doing: leaving one property that was not yet on fire to check out the residents of another property whom they thought were probably dead. They were also driving a car, barely able to see through the smoke, not knowing whether the firestorm would return.

They arrived at the homestead to be confronted with an extraordinary sight. The fire alarms were all screaming and John's mother Pam was calmly making sandwiches. The house was untouched.

But it was not yet time for celebration. The garden was on fire and the mulch was burning. Some embers against the walls of the house were scorching the timber. John picked up a hose and doused them, only to find the same mulch catching fire again and again. The ember shower continued, the wind was roaring, but the fireball had passed.

John and his neighbour Alex drove up to Braeside. 'The car shed was alight and was starting to ignite the house,' says John. 'We needed two people there, one would not have been able to save that place alone.' For the next twenty minutes the two men battled to prevent the house burning down. The walkie-talkie radios crackled into life; one by one every person on Booroomba called in, all alive and accounted for. There were no injuries, no homes burning, though some sheds and stock had gone.

The firestorm had moved on to the far side of the valley but the winds were still strong, the smoke, thick with ash and debris from trees still burning way up in the Snowies continued to drop embers from the sky.

At Booroomba, however, all was not yet well. The trees flared up, shrubs burned for a moment or two, grass appeared to catch alight. Mulch burned, was hosed down and caught fire again a minute or two later. Anna sprayed the roses and the house walls and kept the roof damp. The fire caught the beautiful front garden, destroying the ornamental bridges, and fire scorched the far side of the soaked front lawn. But it gradually became clear that Booroomba was safe.

And Blytheburn was fine too. Now they had only to mop up outbreaks of flame at other homes and sheds. But nothing had been lost that could not be replaced.

Night fell and the defenders gathered at Booroomba for a cup of tea. Everybody was exhausted, with stinging red eyes. Though they did not know it, they would need time for the psychological trauma to fade. There was talk about neighbouring properties. One neighbour lost home and possessions; another couple, fleeing in their car, were injured when the back window exploded and showered them with glass. But throughout the Namadji Ranges, everybody survived: there were no deaths.

Over the radio they learned what had happened in Canberra: four dead, 500 homes and buildings lost. 'John and I thought: If the firefront in Canberra was anything like the explosion at Booroomba, why only five hundred houses?' says Anna.

Next day John set out to check the livestock. Hundreds of sheep were trapped in mud on the edge of the dams. They were plucked out, as they would have died had they stayed there. Most were motionless, in shock. Many lambs were dead or dying, having breathed superheated air and scorched their airways. There was no hay or fodder for feed. On Booroomba, they hand-fed sheep and discovered that some were unable to eat grain; they died of starvation. A friend sent a semitrailer load of hay down from his property in the Hunter Valley. Cattle were assumed to have died, but some returned from the scrub six months later.

Anna used her video camera to record the devastation. The old poplars that survived the fires of 1939 had taken a direct hit; most of those planted for Elizabeth McKeahnie had to be cut down. Dead sheep were discovered floating in the creek that supplied water for the house. The cubbyhouse in the garden was burned, but the plastic dog kennels alongside survived. The skin on Anna's face, which was puffy and hard, started to peel three days later. At a barbecue two weeks after the fire one guest was wearing half a charred stockman's hat, which the other guests thought was very funny.

The cleanup continued for months, even years. John replanted the property with deciduous trees, not eucalypts. The mulch in the garden was graded away, never to be placed around the house again. John bought more buckets: about thirty per house, he thought. Buckets of water are often more effective than hoses in controlling spot fires. John made the dam out the front of the house even bigger so helicopters could take water from it.

John never stops thinking about the 2003 fire. He's planning for the next one.

SIX

SCHOOL'S OUT

The small town of Toongabbie is in Gippsland, Victoria, 150 kilometres east of Melbourne and twenty-five kilometres north of Traralgon. The next village is Cowwarr, a collection of buildings, a shop and a hotel about eight kilometres away to the east. Cowwarr Weir, the local swimming hole, lies between the two towns, with a scattering of a few houses. The country is mostly green pasture, suitable for dairying and hay production. The Victorian Alps start here, where the flat paddocks quickly yield to the hilly state forest and alpine wilderness. The sea is to the southeast, millions of hectares of eucalypt forest stretch to the northwest.

It is a popular area. People have come to the area because of its natural beauty. The foothills of the Alps have views across the plains, but on three sides there is heavy growth of native mountain trees: messmates, stringybark, silver top, grey box, ironbark. There is something flinty and appropriate about these names. This country looks wealthy, but it is not: there are only two centimetres of topsoil covering clay sediment. But it is beautiful.

In Wykes Road, Toongabbie, lived Kirsten McIndoe and her family. They moved there from Victoria's west coast in 1997 and built a mud-brick and corrugated-iron home high up in the hills, surrounded by forest. The idea of bushfires was uppermost in their minds and Kirsten had a fortress built, with sprinklers on the roof that could spray water in any wind across the roof and at least two metres out from the verandas. The family learned all they could about fire and its behaviour: they regularly attended community meetings intended to make all residents fire-ready.

About 500 metres down the hill lived a bloke known as 'the old timer' (he did not wish to be further identified for this book). He was a loner whose wife's death took from him his lifelong friend and companion. He lived by himself in a cedar house on stumps. He had installed cheap black plastic poly pipe under his veranda eaves and another loop under the floor; every three metres or so he had inserted a cheap plastic sprinkler. The system was fed by a small petrol-powered pump attached to a normal household tank. Up on the roof were three copper sprinklers as well. Several two-inch fire hoses were coiled out the front of the house; they could be used if attached to a fire truck, but he had never used them. Two backpacks capable of carrying about twenty litres of water were out the front of the house too, unused.

The old timer's main protection was common sense. He had no shrubbery around his house, his tank or shed. He regularly cleaned up every piece of bark, every leaf, twig or branch that fell at the foot of the hundred or so giant silver-top eucalypts that grew near his house, and wondered why other people in the district did not do the same.

Yet another approach to the constant danger of bushfire was adopted by Sue Coppock and her family. They lived on five hectares – with three dams and a couple of cows — about a kilometre northeast of the McIndoes. Mick Coppock took the threat of fire very seriously, and had drilled his family in procedures. There was a firebox on the front porch with personal safety equipment, goggles, masks, torches, water bottles and gloves. On the lid Mick had painted a map showing how the water system would work if a bushfire threatened the property. Told that plastic pipe would melt during a bushfire, he dug channels and buried all the pipes.

Sue was somewhat sceptical about all this. 'He showed us how it all worked, and how to change the water flow to other hoses,' she says. 'He was a bit obsessed about it all. He told us to make sure the grass around the pumps was kept watered in a fire or the pumps would burn.' The hoses were connected to the house water supply, which ran off town power, while the pump sucked water out of the dam. The valve system could be manipulated to ensure the flow of water to the garden taps and tanks if the town power failed. 'We had gone through the plan and decided if all else failed we'd be okay in the dam,' says Sue.

The Savige family, consisting of Maureen and her two teenage girls Laura and Courtney, attended the Toongabbie community meetings and had their own fire plan. They moved two precious animals, Picadream, a thoroughbred dressage horse and Freckles, a quarterhorse, to Moe thirty kilometres away. In December 2006, they spent time clearing the property of debris. Sixteen-year-old Laura resented this intrusion on her school holidays. 'I learned to drive a manual car by taking those loads to the tip, with Mum alongside,' she says. 'I was well and truly over it all.'

December was a searingly hot month, with clear skies day after day: it seemed the sky had forgotten how to rain. The Murray River was drying up: Melbourne, Sydney, Canberra and even Brisbane were on water restrictions and the normally wet Victorian high country was suffering its lowest rainfall on record. There were fires in the high country, but the fire authorities kept everybody informed about their path. Smoke drifted down on southeasterly breezes, sitting on Toongabbie and Cowwarr like fog every day. The ash was irritating, cutting visibility to a few hundred metres.

Most of the firefighting equipment was up in the hills, with the firefighters trying to build containment lines around houses up there. Residents all over the district scanned weather maps and listened for reports that might indicate the fires were heading southwest. Fire agencies were all on alert: bulldozers, helicopters and the remaining strike teams were on standby throughout the district.

Nobody was looking for a firebug.

But an arsonist started a fire at 11am, ten metres from the main road at Coopers Creek, twenty kilometres west of Toongabbie. It roared through the tinder-dry eucalypt forests at a pace that almost defied belief. Water-bombing helicopters were fighting the fire within fifteen minutes of the first report, but their efforts made no impact. Bulldozers and strike teams were sent to build containment lines along the southern flank; it wasn't safe to try to deal with the firefront.

Toongabbie was right in the path of the fire.

On that fateful morning, Sue Coppock, whose property was up against the trees that marked the boundary of the state forest from the open grazing country, was at work about thirty minutes away from home. Earlier that week she had caught a grass seed in her eye while doing bushfire preparation: with the ever-present smoke, it had become a major irritation. She left work briefly to see the doctor, who advised her to go home and rest it. She received a call on her mobile from her fifteen-year-old son Aaron, home alone on holidays watching TV, using the Play Station and eating. He had heard of fires somewhere in the district, he said. Sue told him they were not close, and that she would be home in half an hour. She arrived at about lunchtime.

Sue and Aaron could not see the smoke as they lived too close to the hills. 'I realised I needed to take the car into town for a roadworthy check, so I got in the car again and drove out, planning to leave Aaron at home. But just as I left Aaron came out with the mobile, saying he'd been told there were fires twenty minutes from our place. I said I'd just take the car in to get a test, come back and we'd be OK.

'He seemed worried, so I told him to hop into the car and we'd go down to the Toongabbie shops and see what was happening. We drove down the road, and a friend was looking at the smoke up in the hills. He suggested we return home, so we did.

'When I walked in a few minutes later, there were fourteen messages on the answerphone. Then my ex-husband John, Aaron's father, called from Traralgon about half an hour away and asked me when I was going to leave. I said without any hesitation that I wasn't going to. He decided to come out and get Aaron.'

As the smoke drifted across the region and a massive ash cloud climbed into the sky, people in Toongabbie and surrounding areas raced back to their properties to prepare or to gather their possessions, ready to evacuate. The police began closing the roads.

Sue's eighteen-year-old daughter Kylie, who was at work in town, called to ask whether she should come home to help with fire preparations. Sue was unsure: 'I thought the fire would pass and said that if she wanted to, fine, but it was up to her. She asked whether good friends of hers, Wendy and Roger, should come as well. But I didn't want them to come out and waste their time.'

The McIndoe family, also told of the fire threat, were in Toongabbie. Kirsten was with her children Connor and Devan and their cousins, twelve-year-old Oliver and fourteen-year-old Georgina. She was mildly worried about reports of the Coopers Creek fire, and spoke to the Country Fire Authority people in town. 'As I was speaking to the CFA woman, her pager went off. She casually said to me we'd have to head home soon. I didn't want to seem to be too urgent, so we had lunch in the park.' Devan received a call from a friend: 'We have to go home now and put our fire plan into action,' he told his mother.

The family got into the car and went home. Moments later the first embers landed in Toongabbie. Water-bombing helicopters had already abandoned fire containment and all available resources were prepared for 'asset protection', being stationed near homes and properties to see whether the houses could be saved. Toongabbie township was the highest priority.

Kirsten McIndoe and the four children knew none of this. On the way home they stopped to visit a friend, a woman living alone. All agreed that she shouldn't stay there on her own, so they helped her prepare her property so she could leave, bringing in all the outdoor furniture and pulling curtains and furniture away from walls and windows. They stopped at a second house and checked on their preparations too. Meanwhile, helicopters buzzed overhead.

At Cowwarr Weir, Laura Savige and her younger sister Courtney were home alone when they heard a radio report about fires at Toongabbie. Laura called her mother next door: 'We immediately put our fire plan into action,' she said. 'We moved our horses to Heyfield, ten kilometres away, and started to water down the houses and the property. I filled the bath and sinks with water, filled buckets and troughs outside with water and put wet towels under the doors and around the windows, moved furniture from the walls and took down the curtains.' Her father Mark, who no longer lived with the family, called and said he would come over to help.

Sue Coppock was also making preparations for the fire. 'It was still smoky outside. John my ex-husband arrived to pick up Aaron and started helping us with the usual fire preparations, plugging the gutters, moving the cars to safe ground and so on. I wasn't too worried ... I thought we'd be safe in our block and that the fire would miss us and stay in the hills like it always does.' She discovered that her new downpipe plugs didn't fit, so she filled the guttering with water and plugged the pipe with towels.

The preparations were straightforward, but uncertainty about the fire's position led to confusion. Sue could hear helicopters, but thought they were getting water from the weir and heading into the hills. In fact they were dousing flames that were threatening homes only a couple of kilometres away. Kylie suggested that they might leave, as it seemed the fires weren't coming; her friends said they would wait five more minutes.

Then Sue heard a radio report announcing that the people of Toongabbie should prepare for ember attack. She lives five kilometres from the town, and didn't think the report was aimed at her. The next radio message was that the fires were five minutes from Cowwarr; she lives ten kilometres from the town. 'We live in Toongabbie East, or Toongabbie Heights, which were never mentioned.'

The fire was almost upon her home. First the winds picked up: 'They were gale force, horrific winds, which I was sure would blow down the trees. But there were still no flames, nothing, just smoke.' She told Kylie not to go back into town because she was afraid of the strong winds.

'Then we were standing near the cars and looked to the west and a wave of flame came rolling down the paddock hill. It was about two hundred metres away. Everything went black, you couldn't see anything. I said, "Okay, let's put our fire plan into action." I wasn't worried, I kept thinking it would go up through the trees and wouldn't come near the house. I can't believe how naïve I was.

'I showed Roger and John the map on top of the trunk and I went down to the pump but couldn't start it. Aaron came down to help. He looked for a moment and then reached down and turned the switch to "on". I felt so stupid. Then the ember shower started.'

The McIndoe family did not think they were in real danger either. When they returned to their home on the edge of the forest, smoke was billowing overhead. They checked that the roof sprinklers were working, changed into overalls and cotton tops, removed plastic fittings from taps, filled sinks, baths and the laundry trough, placed a container of water at every door, filled bottles with drinking water, rescued the rooster and chickens and brought them inside. They received a call from a friend who said the fire was only half an hour away, so they put on goggles and wet bandannas over their noses. The fire alarms were shrieking, the house was filled with smoke and it was difficult to breathe.

Kirsten and her mother Ruth wanted to check the pump in the dam once more. As they went outside a great dark cloud rose over the hill and Kirsten saw huge flames: they realised the firefront was almost upon them. It had emerged from the hills, clawing at everything in its path, with outrider flames swirling blue-green across the grassy paddocks, slithering over dusty horseyards, driving on and on, unstoppable.

The house had about twenty metres' effective fuel-free space all around. Kirsten herded the teenagers inside and asked them to work in pairs, exploring every room for embers and dousing them with wet mops. 'The kids were excited,' she said, 'but nobody was worried.'

The fire was passing right over the house. A massive gust of wind forced the playroom door open, showering the interior of the house with sparks and embers. 'We ran down and put a blanket on the door,' says Oliver, who was twelve. 'It kept blowing open, it wouldn't shut. But Kirsten managed to close it eventually.'

Meanwhile, down at the Coppock house, Sue, Aaron, Kylie, Roger, John and Wendy were battling, dousing ember showers as best they could.

Then the firefront arrived. Sue said: 'We saw the flame coming towards us from the neighbour's property. It was like a giant tsunami of flame rolling down the grassed paddock from the west. I kept in touch with Mick by phone: he was stranded, couldn't get back to help. He was absolutely beside himself, knowing that his wife and two stepchildren were fighting for their lives and he could do absolutely nothing to help them keep safe.'

John stationed himself at the shed, between the flames and the house. Sue was fighting off flames at the back door, closest to the forest up the hill. Kylie, Roger and Wendy were dampening down embers and Aaron was patrolling with masks, gloves and water bottles for everyone. 'There was a bit of panic, we didn't exactly know what we had to do,' says Sue. 'At one stage I was out the back and the wind changed. I remember standing there on my own, in total darkness, thinking: Where are my children? I'm here all alone.'

Aaron appeared. 'I gave him the hose and went inside and took a breather. After a short while I went back out and took over from him.'

Aaron was having a dreadful time. 'I didn't want to take the hose from Mum, because if you've got the hose you have to put out fires and I didn't want to get that close. I was scared, but I felt I was doing all right. Then Mum came out and took the hose again. I was really relieved. She looked tired and messy, her eyes were red and she still had a grass seed in her eye. I went back to the fire box and tried to get her a better mask, but there weren't any there.'

The tension was really getting to the boy. 'I went inside to comfort the dogs, and put the fire out of my mind. I filled up glasses on the table so if people wanted drinks they were already there. I went and sat on my bed and relaxed for a bit.' Aaron was struggling to cope with the heat, anxiety and threat to his family: he wanted some time out, and his bedroom was the safest place. After a short time he got up and forced himself to leave the house, to go back into the flames; he knew instinctively that his mother was not coping very well. He gave her his own mask and later explained, 'Kids just have to concentrate and try to look out for other people. When you're out there you just want to get it all done and over with.'

Up the road, Laura Savige and her sister Courtney were having problems of their own.

The whole family were standing in the paddock out the back when they noticed fires starting among the trees on the hillside about 500 metres from the house. 'They just got bigger and bigger,' said Laura. 'At one stage Elvis [the water crane] was trying to extinguish them, but that water had no impact at all.'

'Mum gave us tea towels, glasses and gloves. We were watching the fire and everyone was ready. Then we saw two neighbours on quad bikes race into their paddock next door to squirt water on flames burning the grass. I was amazed they were able to put that out. Next thing the paddock behind us caught fire. It burned across dirt, and we saw afterwards that it had burned down into the roots of the plants.

'The fire skimmed across the paddocks so quickly it was unbelievable. The wind grew louder and extremely strong. It tore a hundred-year-old gum tree out of the ground by its roots and laid it on its side. There were massive gum trees all around the area toppled over by the wind. Their tops were twisted out and tossed on the ground.

'Then everything went black.'

The hillside opposite and the deep ranges behind contained an enormous quantity of fuel. The flames were picking it up and tossing it into paddocks for kilometres around Toongabbie and Cowwarr. Laura says: 'First there were just leaves falling from the sky, then twigs, then dead birds. I raced around trying to put out as many fires as possible, but there were just too many. My eyes were stinging and I couldn't breathe. I felt I was going to suffocate in dark smoke. Everything was on fire.'

Laura, Courtney and their mother retreated into the house, just as the fire intensified. Laura's father was outside facing the haystack as it started to disintegrate, shedding straw like hundreds of blazing candles.

Inside the house, Courtney was screaming hysterically. The girls couldn't see their father and they could see the fire all around the house, trying to get inside. Laura: 'The whole glass back door was being smashed repeatedly by large sticks and debris, which were alight. Some of the sticks were massive. The fire was chucking everything at us. We all thought the door would break and the fire would get inside.

'I had to calm Courtney down, and I could see Mum was only just holding it together. I knew I couldn't afford to start panicking because Mum would be alone dealing with the two of us. I felt safe while I was dealing with Courtney, telling her Dad would be fine. And then I looked over at the glass door and thought: Holy shit.'

There was a huge roar: the haystack was engulfed and the firefront arrived. Laura's father suddenly appeared, forced to seek cover in the house.

'As he came back through the door he was being hit by debris, he started screaming at us to get out. I had never heard Dad shout like that and I was suddenly very scared.

'We ran for the cars out the front of the house. I didn't need to look back, I just ran. Mum and Courtney jumped in the HiLux ute with the dogs, I got into the Subaru and Dad came behind in the Rodeo ute with the slip-on water pump.'

The family convoy drove to the picnic grounds at the nearby weir, picking their way through massive trees that had fallen across the roads. The cars pulled up at the weir and Laura felt the desperate need to be with her mother and sister. She got out of her own car and into the ute.

'There were three of us and two dogs in the ute cabin, it was black and filled with choking smoke, and we started to run out of air. Mum called triple zero. I heard her say: "I know you can't come and help us, we don't want you to do that, just talk us through this bit."'

Four or five other cars, their occupants also driven from their homes by the firestorm, gathered at the weir with a Country Fire Authority station wagon. One man holding two dogs stared blankly as his house went up in flames on the other side of the weir.

As Laura looked over towards her own house she saw five buildings alight and began to think about what had just happened. Her mother comforted her by saying, 'It's all right, as long as we're alive we can rebuild the house. It's only material possessions.' Her words finally broke Laura's resolve. She burst into uncontrollable sobbing and started shivering convulsively, despite the massive heat from the fires and the wind.

She thought she'd never stop crying. Then she saw her father light up a cigarette. She laughed out loud and said: 'Isn't there enough smoke here for you?'

Brian Mellor, a Rural Ambulance Victoria station officer and CFA volunteer, was given the job of driver for a Rapid Response Strike Team in the Toongabbie area. 'We were told to proceed to a house with trapped children and their mother under siege. We'd only gone a short distance when we were caught in a firestorm. Wind like you've never seen was rocking the thirteen-tonne truck like a Tonka toy ... we could only guess what the mother and three children were coping with, trapped in their house. After ten minutes we battled up the road, over fallen trees, cutting up the larger ones as we went, only to find the family had managed to escape.'

A CFA tanker nearby heard a mayday call from another unit, and teams were scrambled to find it. They never did. The driver of the truck, Phil Johnson of Toongabbie, describes the scene at Cowwarr: 'From ground level up about ten degrees the sky was bright orange turning to blood red. The rest of the sky was as black as night, although it was only mid afternoon.

'We were deployed to Cowwarr Weir estate. The main firefront had passed, but we had to ensure that the houses not on fire stayed that way. Heyfield and Cowwarr tankers were able to save the weir keeper's house, but I had to let others go, as they were too far gone and we didn't have the resources. I didn't feel too good about that, but I didn't have any time to ponder the situation.'

On the McIndoe property, Kirsten and the kids kept the embers at bay in the toy room, taking turns to hold the woollen blanket over the door as a shield against sparks. The fire passed over, and there was silence. One of the teenagers asked, 'Is there anything to eat?' The electricity had failed, so they ate some stewed fruit from the fridge. Connor found a jar of salsa dip in the pantry; while he was opening it the contents exploded all over the floor and the kitchen sink. Everybody found this hysterically funny.

All around outside were burning trees and shrubs. Through the flames they could see a Country Fire Authority truck; the crew were looking for people in a Wykes Road house who had placed a triple zero call seeking help. It wasn't the McIndoes, so the truck moved on. Fire trucks with their red and blue lights and headlights were finally arriving to help, but the number of emergency calls was growing all the time. The McIndoes emerged and resumed ember patrol outside, but they were safe.

Down at the weir, the fires had moved on and dusk was approaching. The CFA staff went up to see what was left of the properties that had earlier appeared to be totally engulfed in flames. Courtney and her father returned in the Rodeo ute to find their home untouched, but they had to start the long, tiring process of dealing with spot fires and embers. Laura comforted her mother, who could not move from the weir. When eventually she regained her composure they both returned to the house too.

'We lost our sheds and the fenceposts were all alight,' says Laura. 'They were treated pine, and we'd put the fires out, and come back half an hour later and they'd all be alight again.

'We really needed those fences to keep the horses in. All the hay had been burned, there was no pasture in the paddocks, and we had to hand feed the horses three times a day for weeks. I got really angry with whoever lit that fire every time our beautiful horses got out on the road and were nearly hit by cars.

'We had no sheds and had to store valuables outside and they deteriorated over time. The horses lived in cramped paddocks. I can't come to grips with the gap in the view across the paddock next door where the neighbour's house used to be.'

The Coppock family discovered while fighting the blaze that none of their hoses would reach their stables; they burned to the ground while the family were dealing with fires around the house.

Then a fire truck came down the driveway. Sue says: 'I thought, thank goodness, someone to take over. But they said, "You're doing a really good job," and turned around and left! So the kids and I spent another two or three hours putting out the spot fires. By the end I was totally exhausted and so were the kids.'

Just as they were starting to relax, someone noticed that their neighbour's unoccupied house about 200 metres away was burning inside. As they watched, gas bottles exploded, smashing windows: the rush of cooler air fed the flames and the house appeared to swell with fire. Flames roared out of the roof and lit up the treetops. Aaron thought: It could happen to us.

The Coppocks lost property – a paddock bomb exploded – as well as a lot of bush, hay bales, the next year's firewood, fences and the tree plantation in the bottom paddock. But the house survived.

The Coppocks' neighbour, the old timer, suffered very little damage. Ash and embers scorched the eaves of the house, but it was not destroyed. The garden was blackened, that was all. His silver-top eucalypts were barely touched. 'If you clean up the ground and get the loose hanging bark off them, they won't catch fire too easily,' he says.

Now the forests have largely recovered, though there is less leaf litter and fewer small shrubs. Sightings of animals are also rare. The Toongabbie and Cowwarr communities worked together for recovery, though there are still empty blocks where homes used to be. Some still speak softly about neighbours who are finding difficulty in rebuilding their lives.

Sue Coppock will always be grateful to her husband for setting up the fire plan that saved their house, and for working tirelessly raking gum leaves, clearing small scrub and cleaning out gutters. Aaron doesn't talk too much about the fire, though he looks at a picture of himself in a fire mask taken at the height of the blaze: 'That's your hero, Mum,' he says sardonically. And Laura Savige, who went on to study science at university, doesn't talk any more about the work needed to prepare their house before the fires came. She now says: 'It was physically and emotionally draining, but if we hadn't pulled together and prepared as well as we did, we'd have lost our home or our lives. My life will never be the same again, though.'

SEVEN

GAFFNEYS CREEK: SMALL TOWN, BIG HEARTS

The seven people who live permanently at Gaffneys Creek, in the Victorian alpine country east of Melbourne, live there to get away from everyone else.

Gaffneys Creek has been called, rather unfairly, a ghost town. There is one road in and out, from Jamieson and Kevington in the north, through Al Mine Settlement and Woods Point in the south. The trip through the town is one of Australia's great drives, barely more than a gravel track winding under towering Victorian ash, with glimpses across purple-blue ridge tops, quiet camping sites, swift creeks and one or two crystal-clear rivers. In places the road comes hard up against a cutting overlooked by precariously perched boulders, or it falls away so steeply you cannot see the bottom. There are no guardrails and not enough posts. People visit this country for four-wheel driving, motorbike riding, gold fossicking, shooting or bushwalking.

In 1991 the town was listed on the *National Heritage Register*:

Set in picturesque, steep-sided heavily timbered valleys of Gaffney and Raspberry Creeks. Remains of town strung out along narrow winding road, they include: early timber cottages from gold rush period [the 1860s, the heyday of Gaffneys Creek, with hundreds of people and dozens of shops and pubs] ... Other buildings include a hotel, hall, disused gold era store and countless ruins such as dry stone retaining walls, terraced sites, stone chimneys and disused mining machinery.

Gaffneys Creek does not encourage tourists to linger. There is no petrol station there, nor are there shops of any kind. You buy petrol at Woods Point, the nearest town, and the shopkeeper decides how much you can have: often just enough to get you to the nearest bigger town. The inhabitants of Gaffneys Creek are isolated but not lonely: they know each other, but don't gossip. Most of them live on invalid benefits or disability pensions. Not all have warm family relationships.

In 2006 the town consisted of about thirty dwellings. Seven were permanently occupied; another dozen were often occupied, others saw life on most long weekends and most of those were classed as miner's shacks or lean-tos, sharing a haphazard life with their owners. The homes are mostly scattered high on the hillsides, difficult to see from the road. On long weekends the community could swell to forty-five, but quickly ebbed away to less than a dozen after the holiday was over.

On 1 December 2006 lightning strikes at Mt Terrible to the northwest sparked nearly fifty fires. Victoria's Department of Sustainable Environment (DSE) tried to build containment lines around them but were driven back by the strength of the winds in the gullies. Fire tracks were then bulldozed through swathes of mountain country, the local fire authorities were asked to backburn towards the fires, thereby denying them fuel. This was also unsuccessful, and as a last resort the authorities removed volunteers to the towns and larger properties, where they did a little strategic backburning and waited.

Protecting alpine towns from fires and floods is never easy. Access is limited, water supplies sometimes unreliable and towns at the foot of hills totally surrounded by native timber and vegetation are potential fire traps. The DSE and the Country Fire Authority (CFA) formed a joint task force to deal with the summer fires. But with the fires out of control, all the towns in the high country were at risk: Gaffneys Creek, Woods Point,

Kevington, A1 Mine Settlement and Matlock were the smallest and most vulnerable. A task force team arrived at Gaffneys Creek and conducted a small backburn at the northern end of town, about forty metres wide and 150 metres long.

People in the alpine region know how to prepare for bushfires. Experience has taught them that fires are capricious, should not be underestimated, and to withstand them you need people and careful planning. The townspeople of Gaffneys Creek knew what to expect. In the fires of 2002-3, smoke settled over the town for weeks and though the threat lasted for two months, no flames emerged from the hills and no houses were burned.

In 2006 there was a further complication: the region had recorded its driest eleven-month period on record. The Gaffneys Creek community cleaned up nervously. All over the area incident controllers huddled over desks and computer terminals, studying maps, forecasts, graphs about resource deployment; trying to work out the most effective ways of combating the fire threat.

On Saturday 9 December the Bureau of Meteorology forecast hot and windy conditions throughout Victoria and the CFA announced fire bans. The following day brought even worse conditions, with extreme fire danger in all weather districts, together with these ominous words: 'CFA advises people living in areas at risk of fire to activate their bushfire plan'.

'Activate fire plan' is a phrase regularly heard throughout Victoria in summer. It's the sign for people to prepare to defend their properties, or to make the decision to leave. The fire authorities prefer people to stay and defend their homes, but they know there are considerable risks; in this litigious society, too, they do not wish to be saddled with the responsibility for ensuring that people are properly prepared. They strongly believe that some people should leave early: the elderly and frail, the inexperienced, the very young and people who live on properties without defensible space or water.

This pretty much described everybody in Gaffneys Creek. But there, evacuation was not a simple option. 'Activating the fire plan' meant preparing for the fire. Some residents were estranged from family and friends and would be unlikely to call on them for help. For some people, the house they lived in and everything inside represented the sum total of their assets. Few had the money or the resolve to set up again.

None of the permanent residents decided to leave early. They expected to fight alongside well-organised fire agencies, bulldozer drivers, helicopter pilots, first aid crews and police who would help them defend their town. Everyone set up water hoses as best they could, either from their tanks or from nearby streams and springs. Most placed 200-litre drums of water around their homes in case the water failed. Blackberries in accessible areas were carted away.

Most of the residents had experienced big bushfires before. Peter Luke, known as 'Pass-out Pete', was Gaffneys Creek unofficial fire captain, a member of the CFA for thirty years, although he had no truck and no unit. He lived with his alpine dingo Molly in a timber house around which was a carefully nurtured garden of natives and exotics. Peter Luke's fire refuge was a deep cellar in the stone house next door.

Other permanent residents of Gaffneys Creek were John Sligo, a retired CFA volunteer with back trouble, who had once had to take shelter under a truck to battle a blaze. He had no intention of leaving his house, believing that your house can save you and then you can save your house. Robert Collier, one of the youngest men in town, was building his own cabin out of mountain ash and was reluctant to abandon it. The elderly and frail Fritz and Mary Von Kustoch, the only couple in town, had relied on each other for years. Bob Matthews, who was a popular member of the community, had a lifetime of bush experience behind him. 'Chippy' Pete lived near Pass-out.

All felt they knew what they were doing. The men of the town talked to one other resident and asked him to leave, fearing that he would not have the capacity to cope with a fire, and would therefore be a liability.

Reports from the crew who conducted the Gaffneys Creek backburn raised concerns about difficult terrain and the lack of space for safe retreat. The undergrowth was tinder dry, they said, and fire would travel extraordinarily quickly. Meanwhile at the Gippsland town of Erica one hundred kilometres away the DSE were trying to defend the massive Thompson Reservoir which stored water for Melbourne. If the catchment area of a reservoir burns, it will lose about half of its run-off for more than a generation, and Melbourne was already facing a prolonged drought. It was obviously crucial to safeguard the reservoir if possible.

The DSE called the residents of Gaffneys Creek on Saturday 9 December to advise them that the forecasts for Sunday and Monday were grim in the extreme and to tell them there would be no 'asset protection'. Gaffneys Creek would not be defended. It would be evacuated. Every house and shack would probably be destroyed.

It was a decision that sent shock waves through the community, and through small mountain timber towns throughout Australia. Nobody had ever heard of the fire authorities refusing to help in circumstances like these. 'It felt like they were abandoning us,' says John Sligo. 'We were the people who did not matter. I was gutted.'

The firefighting agencies naturally assumed that the people of Gaffneys Creek would leave. But the response was astonishing. They refused to go. Some did not believe the agencies would abandon the town, others thought the threat had been exaggerated. Trust in authority began to deteriorate.

DSE and local police came to see the residents personally. When Robert Collier reiterated that nobody wanted to go, a policeman said: 'In that case I'll get the body bags', which, Robert said, was a real kick in the guts. Peter Luke was also shaken by what he saw as the DSE's refusal to help. 'They said we'd get cooked, no matter what happened,' he says.

Four people in the village were persuaded not to stay, and they accompanied the fire managers as they left town. Now just seven people remained in seven occupied homes.

By Sunday the authorities were so concerned about the weather forecast that they came back for another attempt to persuade the rest of Gaffneys Creek to go. They were unsuccessful.

The residents met early on the Monday morning. John Sligo didn't come to the meeting. 'I didn't even get out of bed,' he says, disgusted by the fire agency's attitude. But the others did, and this time they changed their minds. 'Actually, we got worn down,' says Peter Luke. 'We'd had two weeks of waiting and we'd all had enough.' By ten in the morning they had decided they would leave. John Sligo agreed: 'We often do things together up here,' he says. 'Mostly it's one in, all in.' One man, Peter Luke's neighbour, Chippy Pete, decided to remain.

By ten o'clock, a small, sad convoy was heading for Jamieson. 'I felt like it meant turning my back and walking away from a fight,' says John Sligo. 'I'd never walked away from anything in my life. We packed our cars and took off. Some of them took TVs and videos and other items like that. I just took a change of jocks, me dog and me insurance papers. We went to the Courthouse Hotel in Jamieson.'

Robert Collier was nagged by the idea that leaving was wrong. 'I had a vision that I'd never see my house again. I thought a single ember would drop down alongside the cottage, smoulder and eventually burn the house down. I was very disappointed. I'd put a lot of hard work into that house.'

Though Peter Luke went with the others, he was reluctant. 'All I could see was that we were surrounded by fire but it wasn't travelling very fast. We didn't get the strong winds they'd forecast.'

As Monday wore on, the heat in the pub became oppressive. By the end of the day the mercury had peaked at forty-three degrees, the hottest December day on record. Fire completely surrounded the town, which was blanketed in thick smoke. But the town, though threatened, was still intact.

Then John Sligo announced that, after twenty-four hours of free beer provided by the gathered media, he had had enough of the Courthouse Hotel. 'We couldn't save our houses if we were sitting in the pub drinking grog,' he says. 'So I went to the other blokes and told them I wanted to go back to Gaffneys.'

Some of the others agreed. They started to plan the defence of Gaffneys Creek. Their first priority would be to save the permanent houses, and then, after the fire had passed over, they would see what was left of the other houses. But they had no fire truck, so getting enough water to the houses would be a problem. Four residents had access to water in the creeks as long as their pumps kept working. They knew the value of having reliable men to handle the hoses: as many as possible. They had seven. They would need some luck.

The men began looking for reinforcements. Robert's son-in-law David Mahoney offered a hand, which was readily accepted. Eight people. On the way back to Gaffneys Creek on Tuesday morning, John Sligo dropped in to see a friend who lived in the tiny settlement of Kevington. She told him that her son Chris Toifl and his girlfriend Ali were on the way there to see what they could do to help. They were in a ute and had a water tanker with 11,000 litres of water on board. Chris was a drilling contractor; his tank had massive drilling rig pumps and plenty of hoses that could squirt water a hundred metres, flooding everything in its path. The tank could be filled in ten minutes flat. 'He'd be bloody welcome at Gaffneys,' said John.

When Chris and Ali arrived at Kevington it was clear that they were not urgently needed; there were at least twenty fire trucks in the immediate area. They offered to accompany the others to Gaffneys Creek, an offer gratefully accepted.

Chris drove the truck, with Ali behind it. She had a UHF radio and could be Chris's eyes and ears. The couple, who had been together for about a year, trusted each other explicitly, and both were well organised and intelligent.

Richard Stanton and his daughters, Emma and Julia, in front of his Warragamba Avenue home that he saved during the Canberra bushfires.

Melissa and Ric Hingee and Tess outside their new home. On the left is the lane Ric fled down as fireballs scorched his T-shirt.

Sue Coppock and son Aaron with the family bushfire box and Muffie.

Robert Collier and Big John Sligo outside Big John's house. Note the scorch marks on the roof line above the veranda.

Rob Bourke with Taz.

Pass-out Pete Luke, with the remains of the neighbour's home that he and Chippy Pete tried to save.

Judy Causon surveys the damage outside her Snake Valley home.
The sprinkler system can be seen alongside the veranda post.
(*Image by Colin Causon*)

Dead trees tower over Four Mile Creek.

Kellie and Coco take the Gough family for a walk. From left: Liam, Donna, Paul, Kieren and Caley. Their home is in the background.

John, Cathy and Tim McCallum at 'Escape Rock' with one of their dogs.

Kath, Zoe, Robert, Alan, Tish and baby beside the old fire truck.

Jay and Bea Hackett with daughter Bowen in front of the Community Fire Unit storage locker at Mt Ku-rin-gai.

Flames outside Alex Whitlock's house caused by the fire brigade's back-burn. (*Image by Alex Whitlock*)

Ray and Jeanette Bryant's home in Phegans Bay burning. (*Image by Charles Smith*)

Fires emerging from the Namadgi Ranges at 1.30 pm on 18 January 2003. The farmhouse was saved after a desperate battle. (*Image by Peter Hann*)

Crew Captain Sacha Price as the Phegans Bay fire comes under control.

The Gaffneys Creek mob planned together. Walkie-talkies were distributed so they could keep in contact with each other and call for help if necessary. They ran hoses out of the main creeks to give each of the occupied homes plenty of water, and placed a big pump in the creek in the centre of town to refill the truck. Meanwhile, grey and white smoke drifted over Gaffneys Creek; every night the defenders could see the flames on the ridges, moving closer. They watched the fire advance, and waited.

By Wednesday evening the fires were still up on the ridges and the forecast for the rest of the week was for mild temperatures. But strong winds were forecast for Thursday, and the undergrowth was still tinder dry.

'We thought those winds would push the fires into the valley,' says Robert Collier. 'We knew it was coming.'

Paul Bellerby, the owner of a holiday house at Gaffneys, turned up to help. There were now eleven defenders, seven permanent houses and one fire truck.

On Thursday they woke up to a cool wind; most put on sweaters. The fires edged closer, creeping further down the mountainsides. Most people assumed the fires would be driven ahead of the prevailing winds, slowly at first, probably from the north. Then they would accelerate, but not so fast that there would be no warning.

But this fire was different. It defied standard fire behaviour – and even the laws of physics.

The wind strengthened as predicted late in the afternoon. Everybody felt it and the fires suddenly increased in intensity, ringing the whole town. Robert Collier says: 'The fire sucked air out of the valley to feed itself. The air swirled and dropped embers everywhere. The air being sucked upwards was replaced by more air coming in through the valley at the end at ground level. It all happened so fast that the air caught alight like a combustion stove.'

Robert, who was building a cabin on the hillside that bordered the Gaffneys Creek cricket ground, left his property in his ute to see what was happening at the other end of town. 'I saw a spot fire on the hillside that grew very quickly. I don't know where it came from: it wasn't where I expected.' He had the hoses laid out up the hill to his cottage and placed 200-litre drums of water at the corners in case the pumps failed. All he had to do was turn on the pumps at the foot of the hill, check they were working, then drive out of the cricket ground up his long drive, and he would be at home waiting for the fire.

'I turned the car around and raced back to tell my son-in-law David that the fire was coming. I was expecting to connect the two pumps and get the water flowing. I got back to the cricket ground to turn the water on, and was just yelling to David, who was uphill at the house, when the cricket ground just exploded.'

The whole valley seemed to burst into flames at once. Robert described the next few minutes: 'The whole oval erupted in flame. It didn't burn from one end to the other, it just went all yellow at once and blew up. On the other side of the oval it did exactly the same thing, and it looked like a blanket of flame, ten metres off the ground, covering fifty metres by thirty or forty.' Robert scrambled desperately back up the embankment to his house, where he expected to see David fighting the embers and squirting the timber walls with one of the hoses.

But David wasn't there. When the flames emerged David jumped down the embankment, expecting to join his father-in-law at the bottom. By this time Robert was heading back up. The air went black with smoke, the wind roared. On his left David just saw his father-in-law scrambling back up the embankment, just as it was engulfed in flames. David bolted for the safety of the cricket pitch.

Chris and Ali had moved their trucks to the cricket ground and David raced towards them, yelling for help. Ali used the UHF radios to call to Robert, and was amazed that he responded. 'There was a big wall of flame around the house, and we were very worried about his safety,' she said.

'I was putting out spot fires with a knapsack up behind Fritz and Mary's,' recalled Chris. The Von Kustoch house was the first to come under ember attack. 'It wasn't even a particularly hot day, but some embers must have been blown to the foot of the spur towards the north side of town, and they started burning uphill very quickly. Then another fire came down German Spur and the two sort of joined up.' This is a phlegmatic way of saying that the valley lit up like a flamethrower.

Chris was very worried; so was Ali, who was helping him. 'As far as I could tell everybody below the Vicroads shed in Gaffneys was in peril, so we took the truck to the cricket pitch to wait until the flames blew over.'

Meanwhile, Peter Luke was in town, dealing with spot fires. He saw them join up near his house and drove home. He remembered that the DSE had conducted a backburn just above his property, and thought that would slow the flames. He was expecting an ember shower before the firefront, and believed that these flames were just the initial fire. Being self-sufficient and experienced with the ability to think carefully, he was able to gather his wits, and he started to hose down his own property. The fires burned up to his shed, so he moved the pump to the other end of his property and started hosing down again.

The fires grew larger and larger, and Peter's property was shrouded in dark smoke. He says, 'I had goggles on and a mask, but my eyes were stinging. I hosed down for as long as I dared. All up the valley I was listening to explosions caused by gas bottles. The noise from the fire got louder and louder and I could feel the heat from the fire several metres away, and then the smoke got so thick I couldn't see.'

Peter headed for his cellar. 'But it was filled with smoke. And then I saw the gas bottles and I knew I was in big trouble.'

Peter's house was dry-as-sticks weatherboard. The fire was huge and close to the house, and the water sprays were feeble, barely having an impact. 'I knew I had to get out,' he says. He remembered the training that the CFA hammers into every recruit: if all else fails, the last refuge is somewhere in the open with the least amount of fuel in it, preferably with some sort of depression, or maybe a log to shelter from the radiant heat. He grabbed a blanket from the veranda, then remembered his dog. Precious moments were lost while he shouted for Molly, found and grabbed her.

'The biggest cleared area was my vegetable patch about twenty metres away. I ran and lay down and made a little tent over myself. I thought it would preserve the last of the oxygen in the valley for me to breathe.' He thought he was going to die, and was not surprised that Molly did not want to come under the blanket with him. She raced off somewhere.

'Under the blanket I could hear explosions – the gas bottles from the houses further up, and I could just imagine all my neighbours dead up the road. The wind was roaring, the trees cracking: an awful lot of noise. I thought some of the explosions were coming from my house, but there wasn't anything I could do. I thought I wasn't going to survive. Then I thought, Try to relax, there's no point in getting worked up too much.'

Peter stayed under the blanket, safe from radiant heat, until he thought the worst was over. He peered out. He could see two houses, his own and the neighbouring stone and timber cottage. Already the stone cottage was smouldering, with smoke coming from the veranda.

Then, just as quickly as the flames came up the firefront passed, leaving behind flaming trees and embers everywhere. Peter realised that his own old house was unaffected, though there were embers smouldering under the floorboards. Quickly he dealt with this threat.

His neighbour, Chippy Pete, arrived. Both realised that smoke was still coming from the stone cottage next door; after a prolonged battle, they managed to put the fire out. And then, despite fires burning all around, with explosions coming from elsewhere in the valley, the two men found cutting equipment, opened the cage containing the gas bottles in Peter's cellar and moved them out of fire danger. Molly trotted back, safe and sound.

Meanwhile, the town was blanketed in smoke and down at the cricket ground David Mahoney was trying to control his terror.

Trapped up at his house, Robert had no choice about what to do next: 'I hid behind my woodshed as the main front went through,' he says. He stayed there for a few minutes, protected from the radiant heat, waited for the nearby scrub to burn off then raced for the nearest hose. 'As soon as I could, I grabbed the hose to spray on the roof. The fire hose died almost immediately, and I was down to bucketing water out of the forty-four-gallon drums at each corner of my house.' But despite the massive fires, the house was not alight. 'The poly pipe kept burning. I had to save the house first but once I knew that was probably okay I was able to put the little fires out.'

Chris, Ali and David went to help Robert, but the water truck became stuck at the foot of his steep drive. Firefighting was halted for twenty minutes while they towed the truck out. Shaken by his ordeal, David stayed at the cottage, using buckets of water on the flames while the others headed into town. Once there, Chris and Robert drove from house to house trying to put out spot fires. It was hot, exhausting and dangerous work. Chris held the big hose nozzles; Rob wore a twenty-litre firefighting knapsack, which he used to squirt on fires started by ember attacks. They were unable to save the community hall, which had long grass along the sides and plenty of space for embers to blow underneath the floorboards.

Ali worked alongside Chris. 'I was following his lead,' she says. 'We pulled up at the shed maintained by Vicroads, which had a warning symbol on the wall for flammable liquids. Chris was putting out fires nearby, so I went to check the building. Then I heard gas bottles exploding and saw shrapnel landing on the road. Chris yelled out to me to go. I'm pretty cool in a crisis but I could see he was way too close to the building, and I was worried he wouldn't get out in time.'

The last house in town belongs to John Sligo. It's a small weatherboard cottage built in 1990 using second-hand materials and rough sawn timber to give it the look of an original home. The fires had engulfed the cricket pitch between his house and Robert's cottage, and were heading south along the valley. John and his friend Paul Bellarby rushed for the hoses outside, but within moments the heat became overwhelming and they both stumbled back inside. 'When I came in the house I had my peaked cap on, and my hair and the top of my ear were burned,' says John.

His home was safe, but it was no place for the fainthearted. The power had gone off and it was dark and filled with smoke. 'I looked out the window and flames hit the front fence and the grevillea by the front door went whoosh,' says John.

'Sparks started coming inside through gaps around the door. I squirted them with the weed sprayer spray pack I had. We covered up in blankets to protect ourselves against radiant heat and sat in the front room.

'Once the main front had gone past the house, we came out and started fighting the fires. The pumps were already running, so we grabbed the hoses. Everything was burning, the grass, the trees, shrubs, power poles, everything. We started on the northwest side of the house, hosing the walls and shrubs in the direction the fire had come.

'Flames appeared in the gutters of the shed behind me; I hadn't taken off the gutter guard and it was on fire. I wrenched the guard out, still burning, and threw it onto the lawn, in a place that had already burned. We squirted it a few times, but it wouldn't go out. We continued to hose the house and surrounds from the ridge cap to the veranda and the walls.

'I had a hundred feet of inch-and-a-half canvas hose with a CFA-type fog nozzle, which I was handling OK. I asked Paul to start the garden hoses, to crawl under the house and hose down there. The embers were burning right under where I had been sitting a few minutes earlier. We found an offcut of poly pipe burning under the house. We couldn't get rid of the flames simply by squirting water at it, so we had to pull it out and throw it away from the house too. We didn't have time to think about all this. This house is my only asset and I had to save it.

'It was extremely hot and smoky. I had goggles and a respirator and the wind was blowing the water from the fire house straight back into me at times. I nearly drowned! The goggles needed a pair of built-in windscreen wipers so I could see what I was doing.

'Sometimes I was just facing the source of the heat, then the smoke cleared and we could see what we had to wet down. At one stage I saw a neighbour's cottage on fire about seventy-five metres away, so I sprayed water up in the air and the wind was strong enough to push the water right over to where it was needed. But I couldn't get enough water on it to have any impact.'

An hour or so after first fleeing from the fire front, John's battle was almost over. 'When we secured this place I was absolutely knackered. I sat down on the back veranda to catch my breath and the stump behind the garage ignited, so I started the pump again and put that out.

'The house next door that I tried to hose down was engulfed. The roof caved in and three gas bottles went off. That is the loudest noise I ever heard in my life. They just exploded!'

John used 4500 litres of water in the hour or so he fought off the flames, but his tank was still more than half full. He thinks he might have been overwhelmed if Paul had not stayed. 'Paul had never been in a fire before in his life. He was hanging onto me. He did everything I told him, and he turned out to be a champion.'

As soon as John's house was secure Paul headed off into town to help other residents. Chippy Pete and Peter Luke thought they might join the crew saving other properties, too. The water in their fire trailer ran out, so they went to the creek and refilled. When they returned to check on their own properties, they noticed that the veranda of Peter's neighbour's house was smoking yet again, and they spent another few minutes dousing the flames. They went into town and did what they could to save homes and douse spot fires. But embers had got into the attic of

Peter's neighbour's house and it burst into flame. All that was left was the stonework at both ends. After trying so hard to save the property three times, Peter was shocked and saddened by the damage.

The rain came as gentle showers just after eight that evening and the disaster was over. All the occupied homes at Gaffneys Creek and eight unoccupied dwellings were saved, along with the CFA and Vicroads sheds.

John Sligo, Robert Collier, Peter Luke and the others are still happy to recall their actions on that day, but all are saddened by the loss of so much of their town. Gaffneys Creek is even quieter, and perhaps it is a little closer to dying. John Sligo thinks so. 'We lost seventeen houses, a dozen huts and some sheds,' he says. 'The place is knackered.' Despite the best efforts of Gaffneys Creek's unlikely heroes, the town lost much of its heart: the post office building, all the holiday shacks and miners' cottages, the community hall. And, after thirty years of incomplete renovation, the stone and weatherboard building near Peter Luke's house remains a stone shell.

Robert adds: 'I don't blame the DSE and the CFA for not coming. After what we went through, I can see why they didn't want to be here.'

All reflect on the fact that if Chris and Ali hadn't offered help the pumps and hoses they needed would not have been available. Fritz and Mary might have perished and David Mahoney would have been in terrible peril. Chris and Ali brought hope and inspiration when the town needed it most: and 11,000 litres of water and a very big pump.

The rebuilding process that often follows calamity requires motivation from the people who remember why they chose to live there in the first place. In Gaffneys Creek, the biggest assets were not the timber dwellings but the relationships and the isolation. They remain intact.

The day after the fire Robert Collier's daughter, Dave's wife Melissa, added to the GAFFNEYS CREEK town sign the words: 'Small town, big hearts'. The sign is still there.

EIGHT

THE PERFECT STORM

Colin Causon's family have been living near Snake Valley, about twenty kilometres west of Ballarat, Victoria, since 1851. Snake Valley is a hamlet with a couple of dozen houses, a pub and two churches. One of these, the Carngham Uniting Church, is beautiful. Opened as a Presbyterian church in 1892, made of blue stone quarried from the nearby town of Chepstowe, it was built by gold rush pioneer Philip Russell in gratitude to God 'for the fiftieth anniversary of gold's arrival in this district'. The church has a slate roof and tall spire and, situated on a narrow winding road leading down into the valley, it looks as if it belongs in an idyllic English village.

Not that Snake Valley really gives that impression. It's more typically Australian. Gum trees line paddocks, fences tumble along, here a vineyard, there a paddock of hay, nearby cattle, sheep and alpacas. The town is central to huge blue gum and pine timber plantations; most of the country is state forest, unregulated overgrown Crown land good for firewood hunting, motorbike riding and gold fossicking. It is a mixed farming area, but many locals own no more than about twenty-five hectares; several commute to Ballarat, offers work, restaurants and shopping: Melbourne is accessible by freeway in about an hour and a half.

Colin Causon has not always lived here. He and his wife Judy lived in Tasmania for a while, where he worked for an agricultural company. They enjoyed Tasmania, but after a while the pull of family and roots was too strong. In 1990 they set up an import–export business in Tannery Road just outside Snake Valley, built a house and raised a family. Colin knows this country. He and Judy knew that any house they built would need to withstand biting winter winds and summer bushfires.

This is bad fire country. One of the reliable features of weather conditions in this part of Victoria is that hot northerly winds are frequently doused by southwesterlies. This welcome cool change can make temperatures drop more than ten degrees in half an hour. But it can also turn a fire flank into a firefront. Hot northerly winds sweeping down from central Australia can fan relatively minor blazes into infernos, pushing a firefront in one direction with burning on either side. In December 1998, a few kilometres southwest of Snake Valley, five volunteer firefighters died when a freak gust of wind drove the flames from a small fire onto their truck.

Colin and Judy built their home to withstand fires. Everything was planned, literally, from the ground up. 'We started building on a cement slab, so no cinders could blow underneath,' says Colin. 'The house faces north, not the likely direction of any fire. We have a corrugated-iron roof because tiles can harbour embers and blow off in strong winds; the gutters are wide and deep, so they hold more water.' The walls are made of local Ballarat basalt 450 millimetres thick. 'The house is thirty-five to forty million years old,' says Colin, deadpan. Windows are set deep. 'If the house burns we know we'll have the walls and a slab to build on again.'

The house is next to a privately leased former state forest that abuts 2500 hectares of pine plantations. Trees covered all the valleys and ridges. East towards Ballarat is the Enfield Forest thirty kilometres long and ten kilometres wide, separating the rural areas from Ballarat's working-class western suburbs of Delacombe, Sebastopol, Magpie and Newington. A big fire in the Enfield Forest could cause great damage to these suburbs, and to the Brisbane Ranges National Park. Colin says: 'The Country Fire Authority would do whatever it takes to stop the fire getting to the Enfield Forests. It's their Maginot Line.'

Not surprisingly, water is the key to the Causons' fire plan. They do not have reticulated water but a dam out the back and two concrete tanks on the side of the house: two independent sources of water. A petrol-powered pump takes water from the dam up to a tank on a rise just above the house. Because this pump would be likely to fail during a bushfire, a generator in a small shed nearby drives another pump attached to the tanks.

Under the veranda is a copper pipe and sprinkler system. The water flows out in a circle, designed to wet the walls and everything about a metre from the edge of the veranda, and also to keep the vertical posts wet so they do not burn. 'Everybody asks us why we built it like that,' says Colin. 'But water doesn't need to get up on the roof. The roof won't burn, but the timber eaves will if sparks get up there. The idea is that water will keep fire, sparks and embers out of the eaves.'

The Causon fire plan was simple: to defend their home outside until the heat became unbearable, then to retreat inside while the firefront passed over the house, and then to come outside to hose down the embers. The Causon children Cameron and Nicole had the fire plan drilled into them for fifteen years. 'When they were teenagers they could work the pumps and the generator,' says Colin. 'They knew what to wear and where to be.'

The house is surrounded by the soft greys and whites of Victorian eucalypts: stringybark, candlebark, messmate, paperbark and peppermint. A quick glance reveals only trees, but a careful look reveals a neighbour: a house with an elevated tank, some grass and a paddock that runs down to the Causons' property. There is a neighbour on the other side: both houses are far enough away to maintain peace and quiet, but too far to run during a fire.

Sunday 13 March 2006 was a typical Victorian summer day: warm to hot in the morning with strong northerly winds and a cold front expected in the late afternoon, bringing southwesterlies. On the previous day the Causons had what amounted to a music festival on their back lawn, inviting about a hundred people to listen to some live local blues. It was typical of Colin and Judy: the Causons say they 'live life with a foot firmly on the accelerator pedal'. They make music, they travel, they bushwalk.

Colin, Judy and Cameron finished clearing up the debris from their blues gig, chatting about the concert, replaying the music in their heads. They had a long, leisurely lunch and relaxed afterwards. It was mid afternoon.

At about 3.30, in an isolated paddock ten kilometres away, a small fire started. Nobody knows how: the police asserted suspicious circumstances. It grew rapidly in the hot, dry air. Within a few hundred metres it destroyed one unoccupied house, then raced along the bush tracks and deserted roads. Within an hour or so, having damaged two more homes, destroyed cars and sheds, it reached the pine plantations. A slight wind change pushed it southeast, heading for the Enfield Forest.

At about four Colin received a phone call from a friend who lived on the suburban fringe of Ballarat about thirty kilometres away. He reported smoke out towards Snake Valley. Colin looked to the southwest and saw a billowing cloud: fortunately the fire was heading away from their house. He did a quick mental calculation and probably swore under his breath: a wind change was expected, and if the forecast was accurate the wind could push the fire straight to Tannery Road.

The forecast was spot on. The fire changed direction almost before Colin put down the phone. The fire that the Causons had anticipated for eighteen years was now closing fast, rushing through plantations of pine and blue gum and into the state forest, fed by fuel accumulated on the forest floor for the past thirty years.

The Causons put their plan into action. They donned clothes, gloves, masks and woolly beanies. They checked the generators for fuel, moved the vehicles, and started the pumps to water the grounds. They did not consider approaching the Country Fire Authority for help; they were sure they could manage on their own. Judy closed doors, moved heavy curtains across the windows as added protection from radiant heat. As the wind picked up, smoke drifted over Tannery Road, growing steadily thicker; embers dropped down from the sky. A neighbour drove up and urged them to leave. Colin didn't give the idea a second thought. 'Colin, was heading into the smoke over a hill and he had no idea what was over there,' he says. 'He should have stayed with us.' Colin, Judy and their adult son Cameron hosed each other down to keep their clothes wet, had a group hug and wished each other luck.

Cameron says: 'When the embers started dropping in the paddock in front of us we saw the whole grasslands go up in flame. There was a wall of fire, heading directly at us. It was a big firefront. It hit the paddocks and went straight into the trees. I knew the three of us wouldn't have a problem coping with it: we kept wetting down areas of the house.'

The first flames reached the property, embers jumped the drive at the side of the house, and the trees and shrubs burst instantly into flame. Tonnes of wood loaded in for winter began burning near the shed thirty metres from the house. Colin knew not much could be done. 'All we could do was play water where we felt things needed to be damp. You don't put out something like that, there's no way to stop it. It's like standing in front of an express train. All you can do is keep things wet. I wear glasses, and the goggles kept fogging up all the time, so I had to keep putting water into them.'

And then things suddenly became a lot worse.

Colin says: 'Up until then we had a fire with flames and trees burning. And then the light disappeared, blacked out by smoke. It might as well have been midnight. And there was a huge, huge roaring noise, the sound of the main front arriving. As it arrived, the fire changed shape. It became like a liquid, overwhelming the entire landscape. Superimposed were long, licking flames, running everywhere at once. It was a maelstrom of movement, but strange: it seemed still, it appeared as though it wasn't moving at all.'

The Causons retreated inside, just as they had planned. Judy says, 'We had plenty to do. We had drapes pulled everywhere to shield the radiant heat, and we had to keep looking out to see what was happening to the flammable bits of the house, and the gardens. I was worried the windows might break. Sparks were coming under the doors, driven by these enormous winds. We were prepared for that, we had wet mops and towels. We should have checked the roof cavity: strangely enough, we hadn't done that. We were prepared to lose power but it never went off. So we could still hear voices apparently coming from the outside: the radio was on.

'We were in another world, and totally alone, except I had two terrific people with me. We didn't panic. We never had a doubt we would save the house. Surrounding structures like sheds we thought would be lost.'

Then Colin went outside to save a water connection, and for the first time Judy was less controlled. 'I felt very scared, and screamed at him to return. He didn't react fast enough, and I screamed at him again. For a few moments I was really afraid he would be injured. Then he came back in, under the veranda. I could have killed him!'

Smoke was coming through the ceiling light fittings and under doors. 'And this was the time, with fire all around us, that the smoke alarm decided this was a good time to go off. It wanted to warn us. So we shut it off. And we heard a chap from ABC Radio warning the residents of western Ballarat, the suburban residents, to put their fire plans into action. Cameron said: "Yeah, they're talking about people whose fire plan extends to putting a digit on the telephone dial and pressing triple zero."'

'It's common sense to say we must have been terrified,' says Colin, 'but we felt we remained calm.

'We went about the house doing things we had to do, maintaining water and rehydrating ourselves, generally working according to the plan. We knew the whole thing would take fifteen to twenty minutes to pass over.

'During one of these monitoring periods we found one of the gutters was alight, so we knew we'd have to move outside to keep the walls damp. We stayed outside, putting out embers, spot fires, looking for anything that might have been burning the house.'

In the inferno, the fire pump at the dam died and the water went off; Colin had to turn over the supply from dam to house tanks and to switch the hoses. All went exactly as planned. Colin says: 'It was all absolutely overwhelming, a really intense experience to be in the middle of that storm. At the back of my mind I wished I wasn't there, but I was with my family and I wouldn't have wanted to leave.'

The house itself had not caught fire. 'All we were doing was keeping water about, keeping fire away from the structure,' says Colin. 'But we could see that everything outside the house was burning. We just kept putting out spot fires. And then, after a while, there was this weird silence. The fire had passed. What was burning was going to continue, but there was no threat other than from falling tree branches. It was over.

'So we sat down and had a cup of tea.'

The Causons survived the perfect firestorm, but not entirely. Sheds were destroyed. Inside a wooden shipping container in the backyard, containing furniture intended for the house, metal had melted and timber wardrobes were found to be smouldering the following day. Charred leaves on trees appeared to be frozen horizontal, blown that way by the wind then seared in place by the intense heat. Every plant more than a metre outside the veranda was charred and black.

The fire raced past the Causons' house and travelled another nine kilometres before good work by the CFA subdued it by about nine that evening. Six families lost their homes, another dozen lost holiday homes and shacks. Twenty cars and ten sheds were lost and 3100 hectares of forest were destroyed, including 1200 hectares of plantation timber.

Although they survived it exactly as planned, the firestorm took a toll on the Causons. They became much less casual. Colin worried that he had asked too much of his family, that he had risked their lives. He felt less motivated to keep the business going, and eventually retired from it. They held fewer dinner parties and barbecues.

But they became closer as a family. To celebrate their survival, Judy, Colin and Cameron got their first tattoos. Colin and Judy are unwilling to describe theirs; Cameron's is big and bold. It is a stylised dragon, its three heads entwined, which he says is his mother, his father and himself: three people who have been through an extraordinary experience together.

NINE

FOUR MILE CREEK

The last place most people would think of as a fire threat would be Four Mile Creek.

It's a quiet holiday village nestling between gently rolling hills and the Tasman Sea. Fishermen started building their shacks here about forty years ago; they used to catch black-backed salmon off the beach, but that's rare nowadays. But there are still monster flatheads in the mouth of Four Mile Creek itself, and for those with boats crayfish and squid are plentiful. Like many of the small towns dotted along the east coast of Tasmania it's usually cool, even cold, for most of the year: one resident, a builder, reckons that concrete takes longer to set there than it does on the mainland.

The clean, clear surf breaks that blow up on the regular northeasterly winds attract people during the holiday season, and there is usually a graffiti-covered Kombi van or two populated by surfers. There are no shops or infrastructure of any sort, and all water is in domestic tanks. Altogether there are thirty-four homes, with another dozen or so on the outskirts to the north, south and west in the hills.

The Tasman Highway bypasses the quiet town. To the north, Four Mile Creek Road leaves the highway, running past Paul and Donna Gough's place, then in front of Rob Bourke's house before reaching the settlement itself. Along the road there are ten houses, all separated from the beach by coastal scrub and boobialla.

On the corner of Emma Drive, which runs off Four Mile Creek Road to the right, is the holiday house of Ken and Joy Silver, who live in Launceston. Their place is not far from Charlotte Court, which is on a gentle rise off Emma Drive and parallel to Four Mile Creek Road. The houses on both sides of Charlotte have sea views; those on the east are further up the rise so they look over the top of the homes on the western side. Ron Jackson and his wife Julie live on the high side, in a cedar house they built about ten years ago. And at the end of Charlotte are Shane and Mary Gavaghan, with their two daughters, fourteen-year-old Laura and Keira, aged nine.

Further along Four Mile Creek Road and on the right is Greenbanks Drive, which runs alongside Banticks Creek, a tributary of Four Mile Creek itself. Across the creek, on the south side of town, live David and Rhonda Jinks in what they call 'twelve acres of bare paddock with zero trees'.

Right on Banticks Creek is a block, on which there is a house in the early stages of construction. It used to be the holiday home of Steve and Deirdre Graham, described by its owners as 'a little pine dwelling that started out as two rooms and ended up as five'. Theirs was one of the oldest houses in the village, overhung by large trees and with an orchard of apples, peaches, pears and peacherines. It is now a memorial to the devastation a fire can cause.

There had been fires in the area before, mainly on the tops of ridges to the west of the town, though at a distance. Several of Four Mile Creek's residents, however, kept a wary eye on weather conditions, generally speaking. Shane Gavaghan is a member of the Falmouth–Four Mile Creek TFS Volunteer Brigade, which consists of four men and a fire truck holding about 1000 litres of water. Another careful resident is Paul Gough, a former Air Force trainer who has lived in the bush all his life and who kept the area clear around his house. 'We don't have any trees within a hundred and fifty metres,' he says. The area on the other side of the cleared land was covered densely in sedges and other grasses that he thought didn't create any fire problems. Paul is a capable man, who has played and coached football and goes camping and fishing. His wife Donna is a teacher and they have three young sons.

On 10 December 2006 a campfire got out of control on the northern side of Mt Nicholas, forty kilometres to the northwest. It burned to the west of Four Mile Creek but stayed in the hills, pushed back by the offshore winds. People began to watch the fires burning on the ridges, and Paul and Donna Gough started a twenty-four-hour watch roster, in case the fires came down overnight. Everybody was aware that thirteen houses had been burned in Scamander twenty kilometres up the road, and that other towns in their region had faced horrific battles to turn the flames away.

Paul Gough considered the possibilities. 'I felt that fire was on the cards. It could come through here and burn the house down, damage the property, damage the cars. I was worried about my family but even at that late stage, like many other people, I thought it would be OK. If it did come through, it would burn the grass and the sedges, like a lot of other fires, and then it would be gone. I wasn't overly concerned, and felt I was reasonably well prepared.'

Winds swirled around the hills to the west of Four Mile Creek and smoke blanketed the town for days. Several residents came back to prepare their properties for a possible fire, though others did not. Shane Gavaghan who, with the volunteer fire group, had been fighting fires in the hills, discussed with his wife Mary the likelihood of the fire breaking into town. They packed one of their two cars with valuables and drove it to the beach in preparation for a quick getaway. Builder Rob Burke hurried home with his son and daughter, who had been competing at the National Surfing Championships in New South Wales. 'We were the last car on the last boat home,' he says. Having been confronted by devastating fires in the town of Sussex Inlet 100 kilometres south of Wollongong in 2002, he did not want to take any chances. But once he arrived at Four Mile Creek, he had second thoughts. 'It was so cold, almost cold enough for indoor heating. And it was damp too. I thought, no way in the world could this burn.' All the same, he cut back three dozen or so great trees growing near his house, and filled the tanks with water. He positioned a petrol pump near the tanks to run the hoses while his eldest two boys Jake and Josh prepared the gutters.

One group of residents got together with chainsaws and cut down the big bluegums separating the Tasman Highway from the main village. About twenty trees were brought down and a wide firebreak was cleared along the fences behind Charlotte Court.

Gerald Aulich, a respected Tasmanian Fire Service volunteer and former fire captain in the nearby town of St Marys, came down to talk to local residents about preparation. He did not mince words, telling local volunteer Shane Gavaghan that 'all hell could break loose'.

On Thursday 14 December, the weather came in from the west. The fire agencies realised that, with a wind change predicted for mid afternoon, the fires would swing around and head straight for the town.

Gerald Aulich visited the town that morning. 'He said we'd be okay for a few hours, but I had a very uneasy feeling,' says Donna Gough. The Goughs packed pictures, clothes, doonas and other belongings into one of their cars, and gathered the boots, long pants and jumpers they would need to confront the fire. 'My neighbour said she'd put wet towels around the doors and windows and I thought, I might do that too. But then I thought, No, everything will be fine.

'Then someone left a message on our phone suggesting we move the kids out of the town. For the first time I thought, this could be serious.' Never having experienced a fire, with no idea of its speed or size, Donna and Paul Gough remained tense but calm. They watched and waited, trying to keep things normal for the children. 'The kids went off to play next door and when we'd packed the cars we stopped and had a coffee,' says Donna. 'But the wind changed exactly as predicted. We heard a whistling sound and thought: This is it, it's coming.'

'You could feel the air go drier within minutes,' says Paul. 'Something was different, you could feel it: whether it was the humidity or the air pressure I don't know. It was nasty, primeval: the hair on the back of my neck stood on end.'

Shane Gavaghan and the TFS volunteers were up near the main road when the first spot fires landed. 'She's on,' they said, put out an urgent call to the TFS and headed straight back to town. Shane Gavaghan's crew went up to Charlotte Court and told his wife Mary and two daughters to leave immediately. They ran down to the beach, got in the car they had left there and took off.

Police administrative officer Kate Parish of Hobart, who was in Scamander, fielded the call for volunteer TFS crews – she admits she had never heard of Four Mile Creek — and set off with a crew led by Aaron Skipworth. The task force consisted of two small four-wheel drives and about five tankers of different sizes. They raced for Four Mile Creek twenty minutes away, shepherded by increasingly urgent radio calls from helicopters overhead. They put the fire siren on but as they approached the town the wind was roaring so strongly that nobody heard it. Black and white choking smoke was covering the town and driving on the roads was becoming very dangerous indeed.

Paul Gough asked two of his friends, Matt Bennell and Scott Gray, to come over and help him fight the fire. But already it was roaring through the trees, heading directly for the Goughs' house, with the TFS taskforce at least five minutes away.

Paul was in the yard when the fire emerged; Donna and the kids were next door. Donna wasn't ready. 'I had a vision that the fire would come, and I'd take the kids to the beach and after it had all burned we would return and put out spot fires with wet towels. I knew it would be scary but we'd be all right ... we also expected we could come inside if we needed to.

'But we weren't expecting the ferocity of the fire. It was amazing.'

The careful plans to dress properly, with boots and long pants, were never put into action. Donna raced to the house and grabbed the pet kelpie, Kellie, and was able to get some long pants and boots from the pile she had prepared earlier. She didn't have time to get any for six-year-old Kieran, who spent the whole day in bare feet, having lost his thongs. Donna and the boys jumped into the car and headed for the beach. The family disappeared into the smoke.

At the same time Paul, Scott and Matt met in the yard, which was about to be covered in flames. Paul would have liked to get inside the house. 'If we'd had time and realised what was going to happen, we could have come in and had a nice cup of coffee while the fire burnt around us,' says Paul. 'We were preparing to fight it with the hoses: we had them on four points of the house, including two facing the fire, and we still had power. But we knew we couldn't physically make it inside. We were confronted by something far bigger than we could manage, and we quickly realised there was nothing we could do to fight the fire.'

In a moment the house was doused in flames thirty metres high, roaring and twisting and hot enough to melt metal. 'Conditions were so bad, the fire was so hot, the wind blowing so hard that we just had to run for cover.'

Paul raced for his old Ford ute about ten metres away. 'The last time I saw Scott and Matt they were on hands and knees against the Besser block foundation wall of the house, shielding their faces as well as they could, trying to get under the house.

'By the time I got into the ute the fire was level with me. It was orange tinged with blue, and the smoke was grey and black, and the air was filled with red embers and the wind was howling. I drove the car to a cleared patch about fifty metres away; I sort of knew where it was even though I couldn't see a thing.

'Then I realised I couldn't breathe and thought: I have to get out of here. I needed to head down the driveway. But there's a culvert in the driveway, which I couldn't see, and I thought, Oh well, this is going to wreck the suspension, so goodbye ute.

'I had nearly got to it when a fire truck came out of the smoke and ran into the front of me!'

The ute, damaged on the front quarter, ground to a halt. The fire officer got out of the truck and ran to Paul: 'I was fearful for my life at that stage because the windscreen had cracked and the cabin was filled with smoke. I thought: This is not good. I am in big, big trouble.

'I jumped out and immediately my right trouser leg caught fire; the truck driver helped me pat that out. Flames were right on the ute. I jumped into the fire vehicle and we backed down the drive about twenty metres, and I realised we were heading out, I said, "I've got two mates in the house." We drove forward and nearly hit the wrecked ute again.'

As they arrived Matt and Scott emerged from under the house. 'I ran to get the water and started attacking the fires all around the house; we hadn't realised, but the house itself wasn't on fire at all. So that meant the fire truck could leave, and Scott and Matt ran next door where the neighbour's house was in imminent danger of catching alight.'

At the same time Donna and the three boys arrived at the beach. Together they got out of the car and raced to the water's edge, ahead of flames that ignited the scrub; they sheltered briefly near some rocks as the flames went over their heads. Jo Burke and her two children arrived and as a group they tried to walk to the southern side of the beach, away from the fire, against gale force winds and radiant heat. They were unable to see further than a couple of metres. Donna says: 'The wind was amazing, flames twice the height of houses were coming at us and the heat was intense. You had to turn towards the sea to get a decent breath. It was like walking through honey.'

Her son Liam, ten at the time, recalls: 'All around it was white from the sand, and ash from the fire and flames and the sky was red. We covered our eyes with our hands to keep the sand out. Kellie our dog was in the lead.'

'I was running on adrenalin,' says Donna. 'I suggested we all hold hands: one of the neighbour's children was really suffering.'

The group edged their way up the beach, sometimes retreating to the water, against the flames. 'When we got to the end of the beach we all hugged,' says Donna.

'We looked back and saw the helicopters dumping water on the fire. They seemed to have no effect on the flames at all.' The fire had not quite finished with the group on the beach, either. 'The heat drove us off the beach behind some rocks. As we were standing there the fire and smoke cleared a little, though they were still completely covering the town. We had to move again, to rocks further up the beach that provided better shelter. They were closer to a police roadblock. When we arrived I asked the police what they wanted us to do and they said, "Get out of here."'

A passing woman gave Donna and the kids and Kellie a lift to Scamander. 'When we arrived the people were all in the street going about their business,' says Donna. 'As if nothing was happening.'

Rob Burke and his family had been in their two-storeyed home on Four Mile Creek Road overlooking the water. 'The wind had been onshore and quite cool all morning,' says Robert. 'As soon as it changed the temperature was unbelievable and the wind speed increased tenfold. It gained such strength and power that the firefront travelled the kilometre from the highway to our house in no time flat.

'We didn't even get to see smoke. The first thing we saw was a wall of flame about fifteen metres high, as tall as the tops of the trees, coming towards us.' Rob's wife Jo, his daughter Sophie and son Patrick had run to the beach, arriving at the water's edge just as the front came through.

'The fire burnt through the dunes and everything on the beach as well,' says Jo Burke. 'We thought the only safe place was in the water, but then we discovered that fire bombs can reach you there as well, so afterwards I wondered if there was any safe place.' Later a firefighter reported: 'The fireball rolled right out over the ocean, a hundred metres or so.'

'My three older sons, two friends and I all had to retreat and get inside the house before we were cooked,' says Rob. 'It was the quickest decision we've ever had to make in our lives. We came in the back and no sooner got inside than the flames started hitting the side of the house and going over the top. Within minutes the garage was on fire. It was nice to get inside, and we felt safe for the moment. But then we thought the house could burn with us all in it.'

The front part of Rob and Jo's house has cathedral ceilings with windows about six metres high to take advantage of the view to the breakers. But now they couldn't see a thing outside the house. 'The flames were going down both sides of the house,' says Rob. 'It was amazing, but terrifying. The windows quickly became blackened by the smoke and then we couldn't see out the windows. Still, for the moment it was a refuge.

'Then I did something bloody stupid.

'The house was starting to catch fire outside so I went to put the fire out. I didn't need to do that just then, but there were flames everywhere and trees falling over. I was thinking: What the hell's going on here? Are we going to get out of this or not?

'I opened a door. The house immediately filled with smoke and the alarms went off. We couldn't tell if the house was on fire or not. If I'd gone out the back I would have been right, but you do things without thinking. I put the fire out where it had caught the house and came back inside. It was now extremely hard to breathe.

'The smoke alarms were going ballistic, so we ripped them off the walls to stop the noise, and every now and then a couple of kids would go upstairs to make sure nothing was on fire up there. Everyone did everything they could. We were scared witless, but we did what we had to do.'

At this moment the Tasmanian Fire Brigade task force arrived. The trucks drove straight past Rob's house; the smoke was so thick they couldn't see what was happening. Kate Parish, driving the last truck in the convoy, could see no further than the bumper bar of the truck in front. 'It was like driving with a blindfold. I had never heard of Four Mile Creek, had no idea where it was or what sort of town, or what the roads were like. When guy in front of me turned, I turned. When he stopped, I stopped. I was frightened. The only thing that kept me going was the thought that I was there to do a job.'

So the fire task force had no idea of the drama going on in the smoke beside them. The trees around Rob Burke's house were now fully alight. Rob says: 'We huddled inside for another ten minutes until the full force of the fire had come through; then, though everything was on fire, it was certainly safe to go outside. There was nothing left. All the ground and grass had been completely burned, the power lines were down and all the poles were burned.' One of the boys was wearing an industrial breathing mask to keep the embers out. He discovered it was impossible to breathe, but before he could throw it away the edges melted and he seared his windpipe. He had a sore throat for weeks.

The shed, eight metres from the house, exploded: 'Nothing would have stopped it,' says Rob. In the driveway an old Mercedes belonging to one of the boys had begun to melt in the flames. 'The buckets we had strategically placed around the house came in quite handy, although those near the bushes melted down to their own waterline. The ones in the open remained intact. All the hoses on my petrol pump burned and we couldn't use it, so we just used buckets of water the whole time.'

When the fury of the fire had ebbed, Rob went looking for Jo and the kids. He ran the length of the beach to the north, about a kilometre, and found nobody; he turned and ran back to the south, another two kilometres. On soft sand this is not easy, especially after a battle with fires and choking smoke. Rob couldn't find Jo or the kids, and was becoming really worried. He turned for home, and just after he arrived the phone rang. It was Jo, calling from Scamander, and she told him what had happened on the beach. 'We got through the whole thing unscathed,' says Rob, but as he recalls the events of that day he looks tired and drawn.

The small local fire crew with Shane Gavaghan saw a house start to burn at the northern end of town and drove up, placing their truck between a caravan and an A-framed home. They rolled a hose out, but something was wrong: 'It was vulcanised,' says Shane. 'Hard as a rock and flat as a tack. You're supposed to roll new hoses out and check them but we hadn't done that. So water couldn't get through it. But the other hose worked. We made a stand and used foam, which sticks better and doesn't slide off. Just as we got foam onto the side of the house, the caravan exploded and went up like a puff of smoke.

'We were all out of the ute at that stage, and the firefront came over: we jumped the fence to get away. We hosed each other and the truck just to be safe.' The crew headed for the river to refill its tank, then set off again, this time to Greenbanks Drive.

The task force from Scamander had now arrived. Most of the convoy drove to the creek, directed by the helicopters. However, the last truck in line, driven by Aaron and Kate, was asked to head for Greenbanks Drive. There they found a two-storey holiday shack belonging to Steve and Deirdre Graham, who had not returned to defend their property.

'The windows were exploding, the house was fully engulfed,' says Kate. 'The whole place was well past saving. It burned down incredibly quickly.' The Graham shack was a forty-year-old timber structure, not built to withstand fire, at the foot of a valley surrounded by mature trees. It held many happy memories for three generations of the Graham family, but for a fire like this it was nothing but kindling.

The local crew, who had recognised that this house could not be saved, went on to the house at the top of the hill, which had a granny flat close by. 'The balcony of the flat had just caught alight, so we decided to save the house from the fire and let the flat burn,' says Shane.

The two volunteer crews, including Kate and Shane, fought to save the property. Kate looked around to see if there was any way of getting the water out of the tanks close to the house. 'We had no idea if there were people in the house and we didn't check, we had no time,' says Kate. 'There was an old fibro shed too, and we didn't know if there were chemicals in it.' In fact the shed was full of newspapers stacked two metres high. It didn't stand a chance, so they left it.

Kate looked in another garden shed to see if there were tools for breaking into the water pipe connecting the tank and the house. The idea was that the water could be pumped from a bucket into the tank of the fire truck and used to douse flames around the house. 'We'd trained to do this,' says Kate, 'but you never think you're going to use it. After about thirty seconds I realised this wasn't going to work.'

The firefront was moments away. Then Kate and Aaron realised that what they had thought was an old lawnmower engine was actually a water pump. Aaron placed it on the water tank, and it worked: they had plenty of water. Now there were firefighting units at both ends of the house just as the firefront arrived.

Kate says: 'We had paper masks and goggles and our collars up to the goggles. In a normal fire you can get to a place where there is no smoke, but here it was impossible. Every breath we took was full of smoke; it makes your mouth dribble. My eyes were watering and I had a thumping headache.

'We knelt at the corner of the house for a while squirting water on it and the tank stand, while the shed burned down a couple of metres away. It collapsed in a heap and at that point I remember thinking: I could die here. I had a million thoughts in my head at once. I didn't know how long the water would last. We would squirt the walls, the tank stand and the trees, then turn the water off for a moment, then do it all again. We had to conserve water. But if we hadn't had that water I don't know how we could have saved the house.

'After ten years as a fire volunteer, I'd never come so close to losing a house.' Kate was twenty-seven. 'I couldn't believe it: a fire in Tasmania so ferocious it was burning down houses and we couldn't stop it.'

Eventually the firefront passed, and all that was left to burn were the trees and shrubs, the tank stand and the fence posts and power poles. Kate and Aaron hosed it all down. Kate says: 'When we had the fire under control and there was no threat of it burning the house down I went inside the house for a breath of fresh air, and people came out! We got a drink of water and went off.'

Down at Four Mile Creek Road, Ken and Joy Silver were working together to save their house. Their house is a cement board dwelling with a corrugated-iron roof, surrounded by a timber fence and with many shrubs. Ken had put twenty twenty-litre drums of water and a full bathtub outside. As the embers started fires everywhere, Ken set about dousing them and keeping an eye on the house. He was protected from the full fury of the fire by remaining inside the fence and down wind of the flames. Joy remained inside, though her eyes were watering and she had trouble breathing.

When the fire arrived on the foreshore, Ken picked up two buckets of water and headed across the road to douse fires at the bottom of the power poles. 'I hadn't even crossed the road when the whole foreshore went up, boom boom boom,' he said. He raced back home and saw smoke creeping up towards his windows. He worked to douse the flames. 'It was really tiring and I was sweating a lot. The noise was deafening, and I was a bit disoriented. You'd think you see a helicopter one moment and look up and it wasn't there again.' Timber stacked under the house had caught fire, and he had great difficulty in getting water from buckets under there. But he finally succeeded.

At the height of the fire frenzy a neighbour appeared, gabbling unintelligibly. 'He was having a dizzy spell,' says Ken, 'and he walked off in the wrong direction.' Ken couldn't help: he was trying to save his own home. However, a little later he saw the man hosing down the veranda of his home, none the worse.

Joy was in no danger inside the house. 'I was yelling and tapping on windows. The smoke alarms went off, but they stopped when the power cut out. 'You couldn't really touch the windows, they were that hot. I was shaking, especially when I couldn't see Ken outside. I was scared but not terribly frightened ... I had always thought I could run through the flames down to the beach.' She did not know about the fate of the foreshore.

The worst was finally over, and embers and spot fires burned all afternoon and evening. But the fire had not yet finished with Four Mile Creek.

David and Rhonda Jinks had a large iron-roofed weatherboard house painted mission brown, standing in the middle of a grass paddock south of the town overlooking the bay. After a year of drought it looked as if it was surrounded by bare earth.

Perhaps because of this, the TFS and other agencies never visited them to talk about fires and how to prepare. But David knew about the threat. He had always been confident about defending his home from fire: 'I grew up on a farm, put out bushfires every summer and it didn't scare me.' He says. 'I was flat out to the point of exhaustion preparing for this one. On the day of the fire Joy was away. I filled gutters with water and connected a generator to the water supply in case the power went off. I put a ladder next to the concrete water tank for access. I moved everything away from buildings, and it was as clean and tidy as could be. I prepared firefighting clothes, boots jeans, woollen scarf, furnace coat, cotton hat and leather gloves.

'At 1.25 the wind changed and the fire came from the northwest. I did a final gutter top-up. At 1.40 the paddock next door lit up with embers. It seemed my home was threatened first. Nobody expected that. All the fire trucks were down in the village.'

David spent the next hour and a half battling spot fires caused by embers, threatening the paddock, the trees, the paling fences and the yard. He had broken his leg in a motorbike accident six months before and, as it had not properly healed, he was less than nimble. 'The visibility was down to about three metres, and the wind gusts were so strong that if you put your head over the fence you got blown over. It was raining embers non-stop, and the smoke appeared to be red.'

From time to time David returned to the house for fresh air. 'Every crack and window was sealed, so the smoke didn't get in.

'My neighbour Peter Allen came over to help me, and while we were here the shed out the back went up. But he left after about half an hour, thinking everything would be OK. The fire-front had passed; David thought he had only to deal with spot fires.

'A fire near the garage distracted me, and then I saw smoke coming from under the eaves into the studio area; the embers must have been burning for some time there. The studio was connected to the house and I realised I had to stop that fire.' But the flames burned ferociously, forcing David to retreat to the main house. 'The glass doors blew out, but I fought on for about ten minutes.'

The house looked as if it would be saved. But after more than an hour of valiant solo firefighting, David ran out of water. 'A firefighting ute arrived, but they ran out of water almost immediately as well. They ordered me to leave.

'Ninety-nine per cent of the house was intact as we left it,' he says. 'I had the house perfectly covered but I needed more people.

'I had to evacuate. I went to the neighbour's house. He gave me a beer and I sat and watched my house burn down.'

The Tasmanian east coast fires were finally contained on 17 January 2007. They caused one death: Thomas James Orr, a local forestry officer who was fighting the fires, was killed when a tree fell on his car. The fires destroyed twenty-six houses, four businesses and 30,000 hectares of forest.

David and Rhonda Jinks are rebuilding their house, and so are the Grahams. Rob Burke is still coming to grips with what happened, and he still feels he put his family at risk. Paul Gough keeps the block surrounding his home clean of grasses for a much greater distance. His old Ford ute lies battered and broken beside the shed. He feels it saved his life, and he is reluctant to put it out of its misery.

Kate Parish went back to Hobart. She is still fighting fires. 'As I drove out of that place I thought to myself, I'm glad I live in the middle of the city,' she says.

Gerald Aulich, who has seen fires over many years, says: 'Perhaps the hardest thing I have had to do in my firefighting career was to drive away and leave people to defend for themselves. Thank God they survived.

'The fire had obviously never read the book on how it should behave: it broke every single rule.'

TEN

ESCAPE ROCK

Cathy and John McCallum are city people. They moved to the east coast of Tasmania, near the town of Four Mile Creek, in 2002, when the words 'sea change' were just being heard. Many of their friends doubted they would stay for long, but they did. Their house, which indeed overlooks the ocean, was built in the 1980s with galvanised iron roof, big windows, wide verandas, big open rooms and kauri floorboards. It was a picturesque house, but the five-hectare property was overgrown and dense bush encroached on the house. There was lawn at the front with a view to the sea over a wide stretch of coastal heath.

Casuarinas, sheoaks, acacias and other shrubs two or three metres tall grew wild along one side, about four or five metres back from the walls, obscuring the view to the north. On the other side the garage butted up against the house and the tanks, just across from the rambling vegetable patch covered by shadecloth to keep out Tasmania's voracious possums.

The bush at the rear of the house was thick scrub. John worried about it as a possible fire hazard, but it was simply too dense for two people to tackle alone. The property access is via a narrow gravel track off the main road that runs along the coast. The only sign that anyone lives at the end of the track is the wheelie bin that John puts out for periodic emptying.

Like most residents of Tasmania, the McCallums knew about the threat of fire. The hills along the coast are covered in dry sclerophyll forest, eucalypts that need fire for ecological reasons. There had not been any serious fires in the hills for a generation, but everybody knew about the devastating fires of 1939, as well as those of 1967 in which 1300 homes were destroyed and people were killed.

In early December 2006 a bushfire started in state forest about forty kilometres northwest of the McCallum home, and it burned for two weeks in the hills. Spot fires broke out from day to day, but stayed mostly away from habitation and property. The McCallums were aware of the threat; they had been listening to the radio as it warned of extreme fire danger and fires in the hills. The radio broadcasts were calm and accurate, occasionally warning of potential danger to the coastal areas, but the

McCallums did not feel the warnings had anything to do with them. The radio advised them to have a fire plan: if people decided not to stay, they should go early. But what did 'go early' mean?

They realised the ranges were a possible fire threat, but saw the shoreline as a refuge. However, they had decided to let their house burn if a fire came. John had once been on a fire truck to the hills outside Melbourne, where he saw what fire could do. He recalls feeling helpless at the time, 'trying to extinguish the flames with a flapper and a stick': useless, he thought, to try to defend one's house against it. And so the thickets of scrub behind their house remained.

On Monday 11 December the fire headed rapidly south. A mid afternoon wind change turned the eastern edge into a raging front, and very quickly fires razed thirteen homes in Scamander, twenty kilometres north of the McCallums' home. Over the next few days the fires burned out of control in the hills, spotting through the ranges. The authorities called public meetings and distributed flyers to urge people to prepare for the fires. Cathy and John listened and watched, but did not attend any meetings. The Tasmanian Fire Service had issued a video to every house in a fire-prone area: the McCallums had misplaced theirs before they could watch it.

As the fires came down out of the ranges, town after town was threatened. Residents mounted concerted actions to save their homes: St Marys, Irish Town, Gray and Elephant Pass were on high alert as fire crews battled the blazes for days; Cornwall suffered losses. Houses burned. Throughout the week firefighters described 'great walls of flame' that threatened towns and outlying farms. Extra crews came from throughout Tasmania. There was concern that fire would burst from the mountains and burn the coastal strip, and towns like Beaumaris, Falmouth, Four Mile Creek and Chain of Lagoons would be in danger.

Residents along the coast were urged to stay with their homes, though the TFS advised them to retreat to the beach if necessary. Still, John and Cathy were only mildly alarmed. Not so their thirty-two-year-old son Tim, who flew down from Queensland to assist his parents.

The McCallums were visited by firefighters, who looked over their home, the driveways and exits. It was a standard visit by the TFS, who try to evaluate the likelihood of people surviving, houses and sheds remaining and the risks to their own volunteers and staff. Cathy and John told the firefighters they were planning to stay, though not to defend their property.

It all seemed straightforward, but it wasn't: the McCallums had many questions. What is 'early'? What are the triggers? Do you leave in the morning or the day before? If the fire isn't too bad, should you stay to put out minor fires and keep the smoke out of the house? When you see fire, do you pack the car and drive away? How close does the fire come before you know you should leave? How fast does a fire travel? What does it look like? Without answers – and John and Cathy thought the situation was too urgent for the TFS to reiterate things they might already have addressed at the meetings and on the TFS video – the McCallums' decision to seek refuge in the sea was reinforced.

Their son Tim had no experience of fires, the bush or farming. He worked with his father removing vines from the water tank and placing them and other rubbish in a trailer ready to be taken to the tip. They moved a large quantity of flammable products from the shed. Tim said: 'We put them in what appeared to be a wide open and relatively safe place, on the lawn at the front of the house, close to the front path.' He packed the cars with important belongings, but left some inside, including the family photographs.

They planned an orderly and careful retreat, deciding what to save. They included the photograph albums, two laptops, the video, Pinky the cat and the two dogs Rosie and Zac. Tim tried to imagine what leaving in a hurry would be like: they would need water, a radio, towels. These were put into a big sack.

On Friday 14 December the forecast was for a mild day with a strong wind change from the west in mid afternoon. Tim and John continued to clean up while Cathy was glued to the radio. Another TFS team dropped in and said that, although they should be prepared to 'go early', the fires had apparently gone to the south, and were not coming down the coastal strip. Relieved, John, Cathy and Tim took a break for lunch.

However, as the afternoon wore on, reports about fires became more frequent and ominous. The power went off. The McCallums brought the pets inside, but had no idea what else to expect, so preparations seemed a little aimless. 'We were naïve,' says Cathy. Peering up the driveway through the smoke didn't tell them anything; they could not see the fires that were generating it. But there were more fire trucks moving along the highway, and helicopters could be heard in the distance. 'It was smoky and beyond the smoke on the hills there was red in it, but we didn't understand the hills were ablaze. We were confused by the smoke.'

Tim, an animator who worked on films including *Lord of the Rings*, had his video camera and continued to tape the events of the day.

The McCallums received a phone call from a neighbour and assured him they would be ready to leave if the fires came. The smoke grew thicker and almost imperceptibly the wind noise and smoke increased and eventually became quite thick – but slowly enough so that the McCallums were not aware of immediate danger. Two helicopters were now overhead and the wind suddenly became very strong. If the McCallums had chosen to leave at this point they would have discovered that the driveway was blocked by smoke and flames. But no embers had fallen on the house.

And then they saw the flames up on the hills. Cathy was surprised: 'They were much higher than I had ever envisaged, up to the height of the big blue gums in the drive. I thought: My God, this is really serious. We watched for about ten seconds and I thought it could actually come down towards us.'

Soon the flames were coming up the drive. John was momentarily mesmerised, feeling that the fire was 'like a little elf, threatening, playing hide and seek with us. The flames were dancing in and out of the bush. I could see we were in a bit of trouble'. He hesitated, wondering how long they would take to get to the house itself.

And then Cathy said, very firmly: 'I'm telling you it's time to head for the rocks. Yep. You take the dogs, John. Let's go right now.'

She said later: 'I knew we had to get out of there. Adrenalin kicked in.'

The McCallum family grabbed the animals, the laptops, the big bag and headed for the back door and the path they would take to safety on the rocks.

They opened the door. And they saw something almost unbelievable.

Heading straight for them was a massive wall of roaring flames, coming from the north along the seafront. All along the pathway to the sea the shrubs were blazing fiercely.

Cathy was stunned: 'We saw a forty-foot wall of flame in the wattles, coming right at us, on the fence line, way above the height of the gum trees there, and my heart just went *thump* in sheer terror. The noise was deafening.' But they now had no choice.

The three scrambled through the door, turning their faces away from the searing flames. They headed for the lawn and saw the gas canisters and fuel cans piled beside the drive. Tim says he stopped breathing: 'Just for a minute I wondered: Would they explode? Would they catch fire?'

They raced through the front gate and headed for the shrubs. Tim was running on adrenaline. 'I didn't even look back when I was running until we'd reached safety. It was panic. I was carrying the computer equipment, the family photos, and I had the camera.' The McCallums raced the flames and reached the edge of the shrubs and the steep section of the path. The video shows flames flaring, massive, red, yellow, purple, and filled with sparks and ash, with the wind roaring.

Cathy was almost sick with worry. 'I remember thinking: We've got to move faster than we have ever moved in our life. It was very hot. We were being assailed by embers and debris, the sky was completely smoke-coloured, it was only possible to see a couple of feet in front of us, and John could only see my feet.

'I'm a bushwalker. I pace myself pretty well. We were just running. I was conscious that John wasn't as fast as I was, but I couldn't worry about that. I just had to set a pace as fast as I could for all of us. And then John said, "Move faster!"

'We knew the scrub would catch fire. We were just ahead of the fire and embers; one from exploding sheoaks caught me on the shoulder. I thought: If we just keep our heads down, we'll get out of this. All we have to do is keep going.

'I wasn't panicking. Under normal circumstances I can be a bit of a drama queen, but on that day I was pretty good.'

Tim was also focused on survival: 'If you feel you are under threat you have to respect what is threatening your life. Something kicks in and you focus your attention only on what's crucial to your survival.'

He was afraid they might not reach the rocks. 'As we progressed the smoke grew thicker. All I could see was Cathy's boots in front of me, and I was worrying about our safety. I thought we could die, there was a good chance we might not survive this.'

The McCallums reached the edge of the cliff face, and they did not hesitate. They bolted down the steep path towards the ocean, away from the flaming shrubs. Tim looked back: 'I saw our escape route totally burst into flames. We counted ourselves lucky to get to that spot.'

The three made it down to sea level, and sheltered behind some huge boulders. Cathy was enormously relieved. 'We couldn't believe we'd made it to the rocks. We were about a minute ahead of the flames blazing down the track. There was nothing else we could do so we relaxed and gave ourselves over to the moment. We were sure the house had gone up and we didn't care. It was just a house, material things. We would have stayed and rebuilt anyway, we were alive and the dogs were all right.'

Tim remembers the radiant heat: 'The atmosphere was so hot and dry and crackly. There was no feeling that water was anywhere near, even though we were on the edge of the sea.'

John could see that their problems were not over yet: the ocean itself posed great dangers. 'If we got into the water we'd never get out,' he says. 'We'd be smashed on the rocks like flotsam. There was fire blasting through a hole in the rock and I was aware of radiant heat from the fire coming down the hill. I was looking at dropping into the water which was maybe six feet below, in a choppy sea, and it occurred to me that the rocks are slippery and steep and we'd never get out.'

The video shows the three McCallums watching the flames at the top of the cliff, the fire jumping, flaring, the trees crackling apart, and the occasional explosion. As the fire reaches its most devastating point the air appears to be alight and a strong wind blasts out of nowhere, forcing the McCallums to crouch and grab onto the rocks. A helicopter emerges from the smoke, circling right overhead, and disappears into the clouds. It appears again and again, but doesn't seem to be looking for them.

Cathy thinks it was a long time before they started to feel safe. 'There were little wallabies sheltering on the rocks as well for about forty-five minutes. It was burning all round us, right down to the edge of the rocks. We watched it burn.'

After a while Tim decided to leave the rock and go back up the hill, to see what was left of their house.

'All three of us assumed that the house had been burned down. I was trying to work out what to tell my parents after I saw the remains.

'But I walked back through the smoke and debris and saw the house almost untouched. I was overjoyed.'

The reason why the McCallums' house had survived became clear almost immediately, when two firefighters emerged from behind the house. Adrian Gill and Greg Pilkington from the Tasmanian Fire Service in Launceston arrived at the house almost by accident minutes after the McCallums had fled. They had been driving from house to house alerting residents to the danger and when they saw the wheelie bin on the track leading off the main road they concluded there was a house in the bush somewhere nearby. When they got to the end of the track they found the house facing a fifteen- to twenty-metre wall of flame that had ripped along the shoreline.

There was a reasonable cleared space around the home, enabling the firefighters to defend it against ember attack. 'At one stage the fire truck got scorched, and we had to get the trailer filled with rubbish out of the way so we could move the truck,' they said. They continued hosing the spot fires on burning material closest to the house. 'It's a good thing we were there because you need a lot of experience to know which fires to concentrate on.

'The helicopters doused the house with water a few times at crucial stages: the water fell like mist.'

At no stage did Greg or Adrian feel threatened or think they would lose the house. 'We checked inside the garage where an ember had lodged inside a cardboard box full of old clothes. If we hadn't got that, the fire might have been enough to burn the house down.' As it happened, the McCallums' house was hardly damaged.

Tim scrambled down the path and told his parents the house was saved. For the second time that day, they could hardly believe what they were hearing. The firemen came to meet them on the track, taking the catbox and helping lead the dogs.

Tim edited his videotape and uploaded a seven-minute item on YouTube. So far, about 7000 people have seen the McCallums' run to safety.

ELEVEN

'I JUST WANT THIS TO BE OVER'

When Tish (short for Latisha) Proude was a little girl growing up in Port Lincoln, South Australia, she remembers a fire starting up the hill about two streets away. Her mother, Judy put a fire plan of sorts into action. 'While all the other kids were standing in the street watching the fire, Mum was loading the olive-green P76 and getting us ready. Some of the kids were laughing and poking fun at us, but Mum said, "I'd rather have my kind of fun. If it doesn't burn I can put it all back."'

Fires are a way of life in the farming country near Port Lincoln. The town is surrounded by bushland and flames normally blaze fiercely for a short while, create enormous amounts of smoke in the tea-trees and acacias and then burn out. Machinery strikes a rock or the muffler loses a spark in the dry stubble and suddenly there's a blaze. Farmers with their own slip-on fire units work together to put the fires out, and if they get too big the farmers call the South Australian Country Fire Service and a couple of local trucks lumber out and help. It has been that way for a number of years.

Like many other residents of Port Lincoln, Tish lived a relaxed life when she was growing up. She entered the Miss Tunarama contest at the Tunarama Festival, and won in 1994 (out of five girls). She knew of a young farmer named Robert Proude (Port Lincoln is not a very big place). Tish says: 'His nickname was Stink. Mum said he was a shit of a kid.' Robert and Tish got talking at the pizza shop and after a while they married. A fading note on their fridge reads: 'Happy seventh anniversary sugarlips.' In mid 2004 they had a daughter, Zoe, the second girl born to the Proude family in 126 years.

Robert Proude is a fourth-generation Port Lincoln farmer with a 1300-hectare property at Charlton Gully, about ten kilometres north of Port Lincoln. The medium-sized farm ran 3000 sheep and a handful of cattle, had minimum tillage, continuous cropping of 700 hectares or so of lupins or barley, and some hay for stock feed. In an average year they would get 22 inches of rain.

Robert Proude has been a SACFS volunteer for more than twenty years, ever since he turned sixteen. In that time he had attended about a dozen large fires. One near his property he laconically described as 'pretty nasty', and he says it's difficult when fires get into the sheoaks, melaleuca and especially prickly acacia, which 'burns like kerosene', but most were quickly contained and extinguished.

Tish moved out to the property in 1998: although she was a country girl, she had never lived on a farm. She felt isolated at first but Robert's mother Kath, who used to live on the farm but had moved to Port Lincoln about fifteen minutes away on the coast, showed her the ropes and taught her the Proude family heritage. Like Tish, Kath had been Miss Tunarama, in 1961. Tish's brother-in-law Mick was also famous. He could hurl an eight-kilogram tuna with aplomb, and had been Tuna Toss King for three years.

Tish's new home had been built on the top of a hill in about 1907. It was made of solid granite with an iron roof and verandas on three sides, some of which had been filled in to become bedrooms and sunrooms over the years. The front rooms had high ceilings. There were two bedrooms at the front and a formal lounge at the heart of the house. The house has been added to over the years. The modern kitchen now adjoins an open-plan television room with a wall of sliding glass doors overlooking the backyard and paddocks. There were massive pine trees out the front by the road. An even bigger eucalypt cast shade over the backyard, with branches extending right over the corner of the house.

Tish realised from the start that living on the farm would bring her new responsibilities. 'I had a conversation with myself. I said: You are going to live here, well, there will be bushfires, snakes and farm accidents, so get used to it. The first time I saw a brown snake I hit it with the wire so often that I chopped it into eight pieces.

'So I knew I could face snakes, but I had decided that if there was a bushfire, I would leave. That would be the easy way to survive. I'd take the photo albums, the family heirlooms, the wedding rings, a doll Mum had when she was a kid, Robert's Teddy. I thought they'd all fit into the Commodore.' There were other things as well: Tish is an accomplished photographer and she loves pictures. She discovered a series of large framed portraits of the Proude ancestors in a cupboard, pictures she felt had enormous family heritage value. 'I'd find it hard to leave them,' she said. 'Or the pianola rolls I found tucked away.'

Nevertheless she thought she could leave everything behind her if a fire threatened. 'That was the plan in my head,' she says. 'I didn't talk much to Robert about fires, but I knew he had a plan. There's a division of responsibilities on a farm, women do some things and men do others. I was worried about what would happen if Robert wasn't here. It would be good to know what the plan in his head was.'

Robert had experienced many fires, and he knew what to do. The machinery and shearing sheds and the yards out the back of the house were cleared to dirt as a safety precaution to prevent the spread of fires. 'We've never lost a shed to a fire,' says Robert. 'We spray the fence lines on both sides for weed control and that stops fires destroying the fences. They are all insured. The sheep were insured for replacement value, but not for the value of the wool.'

Part of Robert's plan was the purchase of a cheap, unroadworthy ex-army four-wheel-drive fire truck. It was an ugly vehicle but it was solid, ran quite well, and most importantly perhaps, would go some places that the new fire service tankers wouldn't, though slowly. It held 1500 litres of water and could squirt a good twenty metres. But it was very difficult to start, and neither Tish nor Kath could move it.

At about 3pm in the afternoon of Monday 10 January 2005, a small fire began from a car's exhaust sparks – it did not have a factory-fitted muffler — near the town of Wangary, thirty kilometres away on the western side of Eyre Peninsula. The fire ran very fast and attending CFS crews had trouble getting it under control. It was declared 'contained' by fire authorities late on the Monday, but not before it had burned out 1800 hectares with extraordinary speed. 'Contained' indicated that it was burning but staying within boundaries.

Kath, Robert and Mick Proude all agreed the fires would not present a problem. Robert's volunteer fire unit offered to go out next morning and help clean up. 'The forecast was for very hot weather so we weren't going to do any farm work anyway,' says

Robert. 'We did some early patrolling and blacking out. This was about thirty-five kilometres from home.'

The fire was declared 'controlled' the next morning at 7.45am. The forecast was for a day of total fire ban, high temperatures and very strong winds, at first from the northwest and later from the west. However, at about 9.30 that morning the fire broke out of bounds. At 9.50 two farm firefighters in a utility reported that the northwest winds were pushing the fire southeast. There was little to act as a firebreak between the fire and the coast.

The fires grew quickly and the fire crews were struggling. Spot fires broke out far ahead of the blaze. By 11.30 three large and out-of-control fires joined up just as the wind changed to the west. The wind also strengthened. The fire was now heading for the farms and small towns in the central line of southern Eyre Peninsula.

Word quickly spread among the community that the fire was out of control. Tish, at least twenty kilometres from the fires, called Robert, who was battling the blazes, and asked him what to do. 'He was over at the area where it started and I thought, if anyone knows, he does. He said the fire wasn't coming to us: it was being blown the other way.

'That was about mid morning. It looked scary because I could see smoke over the hill, so what Robert said didn't feel right. But he had had a lot of experience with fires, and I had complete confidence in him.' Even so, Tish was alone in the house with six-month-old Zoe; she called Kath who promised to come over and help out.

All that morning the wind continued to strengthen. Robert, in the Greenpatch Fire Unit, was discovering something he had not experienced before. 'Open paddocks used to give us a sense of safety. Now there is a lot more cropping going on, and fewer sheep, and more stubble. The stubble was fuelling the fire with terrific energy, and the fire was racing much faster than anything I'd ever seen before.'

CFS crews, including Robert's, were very quickly deployed to save homes. 'There were just a couple of small units at some of the houses, so they couldn't do much. I could see it was going to get bad when the wind changed, and I started to worry about home. I called my brother Mick to say that the fire had got away and asked him to go up to the property, see what he could do with the sheep and help Tish.'

There were tragedies. A family, trying to outrun the flames in a car, got caught in the smoke and crashed: a woman and two children died. Not long afterwards another family of three also died fleeing the fire in their car.

Robert's unit was moved to protect a house. A fireball came out of nowhere and with it a firefront. Robert says: 'We deployed the heat shields on the rear and stayed under there, with the hoses on over the top. I thought: We are not going to get out of this. For a short while it was terrifying, but the fire passed over and the crew was safe.

But Robert was focused on returning home, to be with Tish and the farm. He couldn't find a truck or car heading in that direction, and his fire truck was needed to save homes. Tish called him again, sounding really worried. Robert says: 'She wanted to leave, but I knew that with Mick there, and the fire truck, she'd be safe.'

But Tish did not know that, and she certainly didn't feel it. Her husband was urging her to stay, perhaps partly driven by a powerful subconscious attachment to the house and its heritage. But all over Eyre Peninsula the day had turned black.

'When I went outside I knew the fire was threatening me,' says Tish. 'I really, really wanted to put myself and my daughter in the car and get away from this fire. It was terrifying. There was immense heat, leaves and soot in the air, and the wind was atrocious. But common sense overrode my panic. I knew I couldn't safely drive away. It was much too dangerous. I realised I couldn't escape this fire and I was going to have to face it.'

Tish and her baby daughter were home alone, unable to leave and with little or no knowledge of fire survival. Tish forced herself to think as clearly as she could. 'I decided to protect the house. I filled up the bath. I wanted to have water to fight the fire. I wanted to be able to soak all my linen and needed to put it around the window seals and the bottom of the doors. I thought,

If a bedroom catches fire and I've got wet stuff around the door, the fire might not get through to the next room before I have a chance to move. It seemed to give me and Zoe a slightly better chance.

'I was expecting the house to burn down the whole time, but I was going to shelter Zoe in it until the last possible moment.'

Help began arriving at about 11.30. Kath came first. She says: 'I said to my father, who lived with me, that I was going out to Robert's. He said I was paranoid, the fire was going the other way. By the time I came over the hill to the farm it was dark with smoke and I thought I might have to turn back. But I kept going because Tish had phoned me a couple of times and said she was on her own. I saw all these cars going in the opposite direction, and I knew I was driving into the smoke. But I've been through a few fires, and I felt I had to be there.

'The smoke was black and thick and the wind was howling when I arrived. I said to Tish, "Quick, we've got to get water into the gutters." We grabbed nappies and the ladder and I wanted to go up to block the downpipes. I'd broken my leg six months before and Tish wouldn't let me go up the ladder.' Kath had lived in the house for more than forty years, so she knew where the downpipes were.

Before long more help arrived in the form of Tish's brother-in-law Mick and his friend Alan 'Weddy' Wedd. He had virtually grown up with the Proude boys, and knew the farm well. Just as he and Mick arrived 'a massive fireball just came over the hill and dropped out of the sky and lit up the whole paddock for about a hundred and fifty metres. 'It scared the crap out of us,' said Weddy.

'When we arrived Kath was trying to get us to plug up the drains and fill them with water. Mick quickly finished the job for them, but I thought there were more important things to do. We needed to rescue some sheep. This was a former sheep stud and we needed to get a mob, probably three or four kilometres away, back to the house.'

Kath and Tish couldn't believe what they were hearing. Tish says: 'I was shocked, I thought it was crazy. Human life was the number one priority for me. I got angry.'

However, Weddy knew what was needed. 'At this point the issue was sheep, not humans,' he says. 'You have to try and save your stock as well. Mick and I had the fire truck at our disposal, and we thought we had to get a hundred and twenty years of breeding into the yards. That was before we saw any flames on the property. So for about fifteen minutes we tried to run down the sheep on motorbikes, and although we ran them as hard as we could, they wouldn't come. I thought if Mick and I could stick together we would be okay. We had a big bare yard and if worst came to worst we could have gone there.

'As we were trying to get the sheep through the gates, the flames came down quickly in the paddocks on both sides. I looked at Mick and said: "We're leaving."' They had no choice but to abandon the mob to the advancing flames, but they kept their heads.

Kath's view was completely different. She says: 'The flames were thirty feet high at the back of the hill and Michael had gone to get sheep in on the bike. I was running around telling them to get inside.'

Weddy admits: 'I struggled with her at first. She went hysterical, she lost the plot. She wanted us all to get out of there.' But Mick and Weddy did calm Kath down and she went back up to the house. A few angry words might well have been spoken, but they were all forgiven later.

Meanwhile, Tish was up in the house with Zoe, trying to prepare for what she was afraid would happen. The main fire-front had not yet arrived, but it was close. Tish remembered that she had seen some fire extinguishers at the back of the shed and went out to get them. 'But when I picked them up they were empty,' she says. 'I walked out of the shearing shed and saw the pine trees lighting up: the fire had arrived. I ran back to the house and got inside; it was very hard to breathe, to see because my eyes were so sore, even difficult to walk against the wind. I could see the paddock next to the trees was alight.' Tish was not wearing proper protective clothing: she had on a T shirt, three-quarter-length pants and thongs.

'Inside the house Zoe was screaming: she could feel the panic and tension. So I was trying to comfort her, and kept putting her down to grab wet linen and put it under doors and around windowsills. I pulled the curtains down: they were difficult to remove; I gave them a good yank to get them off the wall. I thought: Curtains burn, and the hot wind was blowing so if an ember got in, that would be the entry point. They just had to go.

'I was constantly going from room to room and then coming back to Zoe. It was chaos. I was panicking. I thought maybe Zoe was a bit dehydrated, so I tried to breastfeed her, but I couldn't. I kept trying, though.'

Tish and Kath were not the only ones who were failing to think straight. Mick and Weddy turned up with the old fire truck and parked it between the flames and the house. With the firefront now upon them, it was too dangerous to remain outside, so they came into the house to tell Tish and Kath what they were doing. Tish asked whether she should turn the air-conditioners on. Neither Mick nor Weddy could see why not, so they hit the switch: the big air-conditioner on the roof sucked in a huge breath and instantly filled most of the rooms with black choking smoke. The fire alarms started screaming. Tish says: 'That just increased the feeling of panic, so my mother-in-law and I smashed them off the wall to shut them up.'

Weddy and Mick, however, had a plan. Weddy says: 'We needed to get out and back to the truck before the flames blocked us off, and we needed to make sure we had a sensible retreat. The sky was like midnight, the sun was blocked out, there was smoke everywhere. We didn't worry about the pine trees burning out the front: pine trees are harmless because once they burn there's nothing left. But eucalypts keep burning and burning, you could tip the ocean on them and they wouldn't go out.'

Mick took up position behind the Colorbond fence, facing the oncoming flames, while Weddy patrolled. He says: 'I went around and around the house, checking for spot fires, but there wasn't much up close to burn. At one stage I discovered a fire in the southeast corner of the house, under the eaves where a bird's nest was. I picked up the nearest container, which was an icecream bucket. It had a hole in it. I stuck my thumb in the hole, filled up the bucket and put that out. We didn't spend a lot of time looking for buckets because we had the fire truck. Later on I thought the hose wouldn't have reached the front of the property if fires had started there, and I'm not sure we could have moved it in a hurry.' A pile of timber just outside the fence burst into flames, and the intense heat drove Mick and Weddy inside for a short while.

Inside the house, the electricity had failed. Kath was in the television room, watching sparks fly through the tiny gaps around the glass sliding doors. 'They were landing on the carpet, so I just got wet cloths and doused them. What frightened me was when Mick squirted the windows with a high-pressure hose, and I thought they'd break because they were hot. Zoe was screaming, but I didn't try to comfort her, as I was saving everything else.'

Tish said: 'I was slopping around with wet linen, not wringing it out very much, as I thought embers wouldn't catch if it was very wet. I threw wet sheets over my bed because I thought that if the window breaks and the flames come in as embers, the bed will catch fire.

'I tried to comfort Zoe in the main room, I sat on the floor holding her. When I sat down like that I had a moment to think about what was happening. That's when absolute terror hit me. I thought about my husband and wondered whether I would ever see him again. I thought about what was happening to us, my brother-in-law outside, Weddy, Kath – they were all here trying to help us and they could very well perish. Then I started to worry about the rest of the family, Ian and Helen on the other farm and their kids and what are they doing? How are they saving themselves? Tears were flowing, I didn't know whether I would ever see these people again.

'I just thought my husband would drive back and find a smoking ruin and all of us lying in it. Or we might survive this but my husband might not. I remember bursting into tears and saying out loud: "I just want this to be over one way or the other. If we're going to burn, let it happen." I couldn't take any more panic, and churning and emotion. I was sick of it. I just couldn't handle any more.'

Outside Mick and Weddy were taking turns at the water pump. Weddy was worried about the huge eucalypt at the front of the house. 'There were times when the embers from the tree were blowing across the roof in a shower, and there is an Alsynite-type roofing on the porch areas. I was using the hose to wet those areas down and then I saw a huge branch across the outside toilet. If it had come down over the toilet it would have wiped out the corner of the house.

'The branch collapsed, fell against an eighty-kilometre-an-hour wind and blew away from the house. Mick was a rock against that western fence. He parked himself there, hosing down the spot fires and keeping the outside of the house wet, and he only came inside when he needed air.'

At the height of the fire Weddy retreated inside and watched the embers crash against the glass wall. 'Embers were coming under the windows and it was very dicey. I was standing at the windows and I prayed. I said: I've had enough of this, you can burn back on yourself now.'

Slowly the fires passed over: the house was fine. Tish regained her composure. 'I just realised we were going to be OK. The boys came inside and I knew the danger had passed. I gave Zoe some Panadol and she fell asleep exhausted.'

Kath's previous experience with fires had taught her that the worst was over, but the hard work needed to continue. She headed outside, spraying embers and small fires. She discovered the sheep manure under the shearing shed was on fire and if left to itself would have burned the shed down. She doused it.

Robert came home. His arrival shocked them all. Kath says: 'Tish opened the door and he was just screaming, hands in the air, just screaming. He had seen men burned, he didn't know what to expect, he hadn't been able to get in touch with anyone. And he drove in and he knew sheep weren't in the yards and we'd lost sixty years of breeding. He just lost it.'

Robert had had an ordeal of his own. He had been huddled in his fire truck thirty kilometres away, and he hadn't been too sure he would ever see Tish again, either. He says: 'Driving back from the fires there were dead sheep on the roads, sheds and houses were alight, the main pipeline had burst. I was driving over the hill and I knew the house was okay because I could see the roof. I had hoped they got some sheep in. The wind had died down and everything was unreal. There was nothing left. All the trees, even the ground, were blackened.

'When I saw them I could tell they had all had it from fighting the fire for the past hour. They had blackened hair, their eyes were red and everything smelled. Around the yard there were some things still burning. I noticed the PVC downpipes had all melted and the shearing shed had caught alight underneath. I had a front-end loader when we were fencing, it was a three-year-old tractor. She was melted to the ground.

'We filled the fire truck up and went across to the neighbour's house. It was gone. We put water on the hot spots, but there was nothing left to burn. We checked on a couple of properties.

There were lots of dead sheep, but some were alive. I thought I'd better get them penned as the fences were down and I didn't want them to get on the road. We started to bring in the sheep, well, those that could walk.'

Kath called home, to discover that her father Brewster had been battling a fire of his own, which had burned down their shed next to the house. Later than night she was taken to hospital 'for a bit of oxygen and to look after my eyes'.

After the fires had passed and the sheep were tidied up, Weddy vanished for a couple of weeks 'to let them get on with it'. He might have needed a little recovery of his own. 'We did the right thing,' he says. 'Everything is still here bar some fences, some sheep and a tractor.

'It's all about mateship. I've done bits and pieces out here for twenty years, and it's like a second home to me, so when I viewed the fire on the Monday I had some idea of what was coming. I thought: If it's reasonably small, we might be able to protect the house. It was important to have a go. We've spent a lot of time shearing, seeing the crop come up, and helped get it off. It's all a bonding experience over twenty years.'

The fires of 'Black Tuesday', 10-11 January 2005 on Eyre Peninsula, were some of the fastest-moving blazes recorded in years. They have caused radical rethinking about the way fires spread in farming stubble. More than 145,000 hectares were burned out and houses destroyed at Wangary, Wanilla, North

Shields, Poonindie, Louth Bay, Greenpatch and Ulladulla Flat. More than 300 Country Fire Service personnel battled the fire with landowners and residents.

As the fire tore through North Shields, a small settlement north of Port Lincoln, residents were ordered to leave their homes and to head for the beaches. The blaze raged through the caravan park, destroying cabins and caravans. Residents at Louth Bay were forced to evacuate and seek refuge on a beach. Some were rescued from the sea by emergency services after seeking shelter in the water.

Six people, including four children, died in their cars as they tried to flee the firestorm. Two farmers died assisting the CFS crews to fight the fires. A local schoolteacher was killed when flames engulfed the Shell Museum at North Shields. About 110 people were injured, including five who suffered serious burns and were flown to Adelaide for treatment. Property destroyed included fifty homes, dozens of cars, fifteen caravans, two buses, three cabins, one shop, three vans and four boats. About 47,000 livestock, mostly sheep, died in the fire or had to be killed afterwards. All fencing within about 890,000 hectares went up in the blaze, and 95 per cent of all pasture was destroyed.

Tish Proude became involved in community fire recovery projects, and helps out whenever she can. She contributed to *Black Tuesday*, a book of people's experiences in the fires, helped

ABC Local Radio prepare a bushfire education series and encourages people to talk about their experiences.

'Next time I would have a better plan,' she says. 'Knowing what I now know about protecting a house, I would know what attachments I have for my hoses and how to hook them onto my gutters easily, as well as which ladders are where. I would have firefighting clothes ready to throw on, including goggles for my eyes, and all those little things I know you need.

'I'd have a better communication network so I'm better informed about fire on any given day. It might not necessarily threaten me, but I'll still have information about it. I will never underestimate a fire.

'Knowledge is a big thing. I know you can survive a fire in a house. I thought the house would burn, but now I know they don't necessarily do that.

'I've had a second baby, and been diagnosed with post-natal depression and anxiety, which could be related to post-traumatic stress from the fire. Since that fire I've tried to protect my family constantly, in every way. I know that's not possible, you can't protect people all the time. Things happen and you have to get on with your life and enjoy the moment. So I've been doing that.

'But, you know, that day I never thought about driving away. I never considered abandoning everything. I am very proud of myself.'

TWELVE

PREPARING FOR THE INEVITABLE

Seaview Street is on the southwestern side of the Ku-ring-gai Chase National Park, north of Sydney. At the top of the street the Sydney-Newcastle freeway runs along the ridge: the dull roar of traffic is audible all day and night. Seaview Street has a bend in the middle, and here Merrilong Avenue goes off to the right. Merrilong is only small, but the residents have formed a Community Fire Unit there.

Here in this steep escarpment country, dominated by massive trees, rocky outcrops and natural scrub, any sort of community help is welcome. But oddly enough Seaview Street itself has no CFU, a source of puzzlement to Tom and Joy Waterhouse, who have lived there for more than forty years. Tom, now eighty, says there is a fire in or near Seaview Street every five years or so: he and Joy expect fires, and prepare well. They have hoses that reach 100 metres or more, they can place sprinklers so everything including the roof gets wet, they know how to fill their gutters. When fires come their drill includes putting wet bags over their gas bottles and packing valuables into their car. 'We'd be in strife if the water ran out,' says Tom. 'But that's unlikely because we have tanks.'

Over the years Tom and Joy have built up an understanding of fire behaviour, to the point where the actions of some people irritate them slightly. 'Most women want to save all the valuables and little things like that,' says Tom. 'If the fire doesn't come, you have to put them all back!' They don't plan to leave their home when fires come, but they understand human nature. 'Some people just abandon their houses. I have to say that if we were in a rental property we'd be out like a shot,' Tom says candidly.

'If we left there would only be a few men to fight the fires and they can't do everything,' says Joy. 'There are six hundred homes in this suburb. Most of our neighbours stay put.

'We had a fire in the first year we were here. We mowed into the bush and created a firebreak. The council didn't want us to do that, but afterwards everyone followed suit.' Now there is a twenty-metre-wide firebreak between the street and the neighbouring park, so firefighters have access for their trucks and a space that can be defended.

'In 1966 we raised money and bought an old fire truck with pumps on to fight fires in the street. Later someone gave us a tank.' The community leadership exhibited by the Waterhouses when they were younger is probably responsible for saving homes in the street many times: something new residents may not know, as Tom and Joy are not boastful people or naggers.

On 21 January 2007 a fire broke out near the local Mt Kuring-gai railway station. Fanned by strong winds on a searingly hot day, it quickly took off, crossing the freeway and roaring down the gully behind Seaview Street and Merrilong Avenue. A wind change pushed it away from the houses, enabling the fire brigade quickly to set up backburns, a very risky exercise in gullies where there are swirling, unpredictable winds.

Tom and Joy were alerted to the fire by their daughter Debra, who heard on the radio that the park was burning on the other side of the freeway. Joy went out to have a look. 'At first it was just a wisp of smoke, as if someone was having a barbecue,' she says. Debra offered to come and help with fire preparations, but her parents demurred. 'I said, "You can't face the fire on your own,"' says Debra. '"Tom's just had a stroke!"'

So Tom and Joy accepted. Joy says: 'By the time Debra arrived the fire had crossed the whole freeway and was heading down the gully.

'We kept thinking of Canberra. We couldn't help remembering how quickly flames had burned into the heart of the suburbs. We checked on the neighbours who said they weren't too worried about the fire, but we were.'

Teresa Whitlock lives with her family at the top of Seaview Street, close to the freeway. That morning she was at the local Hornsby shopping centre twenty minutes away, and as she drove home she saw smoke and watched fire trucks heading up the freeway. As she approached her home she saw helicopters and fire trucks. She found her home deserted.

Teresa and her husband Alex are British migrants who had no idea what they were facing. 'We had previously discussed bushfires and decided to leave,' recalls Alex. 'In this case, we were evacuated.' He only had time to collect seven-year-old Jake and nine-year-old Lizzie and his wallet. 'We hopped in the car, but Lizzie wanted her pet mice. So I left the kids in the car and got the mice and the dogs.

'I was very, very frightened. The fire had come over the brow of the hill and down the gully towards our house and the winds were so strong. The house is insured. I drove around the corner and waited there for forty-five minutes, to get out of the way, actually. I didn't want to drive too far as it looked as if they had it all under control.' The fire burned to the edge of the Whitlocks' garden, but never threatened the house. Alex, who had been in community fire units in England before, was unaware that one had been set up just two hundred metres away.

Mark Burnett is the secretary of the Merrilong Avenue Community Fire Unit, which was set up in 2002. He and his wife Cheryl live with their young children in Merrilong Avenue. The unit consists of about half a dozen families in the street, and members are expected to attend one eight-hour training session each year. They are provided with a storage cabinet containing a standpipe to connect to the mains water in the middle of their street and fire hoses, nozzles, connectors, spare goggles, helmets, masks, axes and gloves. The members wear light blue overalls with 'Community Fire Unit' on the back.

'We don't fight fires,' says Mark. 'We hose down trees, fences and properties before the fire comes.'

He does not believe that the CFU makes a huge difference, but believes it is worthwhile. 'We can fight ember attacks and the members are more familiar with fire behaviour and how fires work. We'd lose a lot less houses if people stayed to defend their properties.' Amazingly, no other state in Australia has instituted similar community fire units.

Mark was at home when the fire came down the gully. 'You hear sirens on the freeway all the time,' he says. 'So at first I didn't take much notice. My daughter said: "I can smell smoke." I went to have a look and saw the black smoke and thought: Oh shit, I'd better get myself organised.

'I've got a good firebreak behind the house. My plan was to get anything flammable out of the shed, fill up the bath and sinks with water. I know there is an issue of ember attack with my house, and there is a gap at the top of the garage door.

'The fire was already moving down the hill. Once the kids saw that, they started to panic and were fighting with each other. They were no use to me as spot fire checkers. The wind changed and the fires went across the park away from the house. The firies started backburning behind the house. A wind gust came in the other direction and the fire started burning back towards my fence. A helicopter saw that and dumped water on it and it went out. Completely.'

Bea Hackett, who lives further down the hill with husband Jay and their children Bowen and Phoenix, is a member of the CFU. 'There have been several fires in the thirteen years we've been in the house,' says Bea. The house has improved fire safety protection with metal fly screens, the firebreak out the back and hoses that reach to the perimeter.

When the January 2007 fires threatened their home, Bea was out shopping. Eleven-year-old Bowen had gone to a friend's house and, while there, heard the fire engines. She called Bea, who came straight home. The freeway was blocked with emergency vehicles and sightseers, and someone had called her to say they could see the helicopters dropping water near the Hacketts' house.

'We all felt less panicked and less scared because we were prepared. The training mentally prepares you as well,' says Bea.

Still, she was surprised by the thickness of the smoke and found difficulty in breathing. The fire brigade backburned and prevented the fire crossing the firebreak, but Bea and other members of the CFU had to check for spot fires for the rest of the night and the next day.

Judy Lightowler is the CFU co-ordinator in Merrilong Avenue. 'About three-quarters of the people in the street are members,' she says. 'We are supplied with blue overalls, boots, gloves, goggles and helmets. In the early years the fire brigade came to the street for training, but we now run our own training sessions and there are big training days held by the fire brigade at the showgrounds.

'We are taught how to open the fire hydrant access cover, check for spiders, place the standpipe and connect the two outlets and the fire hoses.'

Over the years the equipment supplied by the fire brigade has been supplemented. There are swimming pools in the street so the residents have bought two Davey water pumps and more hoses. 'We got a grant of $2000 for a second standpipe, so we have eight hoses,' says Judy.

Judy is a physiotherapist with a penchant for travel and adventure. She is an excellent CFU leader. 'I assume we are going to have fires every year, and drive my family nuts preparing for them,' she says. 'I'm good in a crisis. The bigger the crisis, the less I panic. My father taught me to expect change: he was very active. He died in a blizzard while mountain climbing, doing something he loved.'

Being good in a crisis is a prerequisite for living on the edge of the park. There are scorch marks in Judy's backyard only metres from her back door, where previous fires have come through.

'In January 1983 when I was eight months pregnant a fire burned to the back door. My family was visiting from England, and the fire brigade arrived as everything was burning. I asked what I could do as I had old people there. They said, "If you are not going to panic you should stay here and help save the house." I got everything prepared – buckets of water in every room, the bath, sinks and saucepans filled with water. The fire burned down the clothes line which was five metres from the back door, but didn't come any further. I lost the clothesline again when a backburn went wrong in 1989.

'I was here in June 2000, which was terrible. It was a freezing winter's day; I wouldn't have dreamed a fire could get out of control on a very cold, airless day in the middle of winter.'

The first real test of the CFU's new equipment came in January 2007.

'I heard siren after siren on the Sunday afternoon,' says Judy, 'and I immediately thought of bushfire because it was forty-five degrees Celsius and blowing a gale. I stood out on the balcony and looked at the whole horizon but couldn't see or smell any smoke. The sirens didn't let up and I was just about to turn and come in when whoosh, it came over the horizon of the hill opposite.

'About fifty feet of gold and black shot up in the air over the hill and I immediately thought: I've got a bushfire. Then I thought: No I don't. I went straight into denial because I didn't want it. It was so monstrous. Then I thought: Yes I do. I've been in other bushfires that were not so huge or so close, and this one was coming straight towards me. I thought two houses near me would definitely go.

'I rang the fire brigade team leader and said: "Do you realise we have a fire?" I knew they must have known, but they were on the other side of the hill and I wanted them to know it had got away.

'I started ringing around. The first person I called was a visitor in charge of a child's birthday party. I explained what was happening and said: "I suggest you get out straight away." And they did. They just dropped the party and all those cars went up the hill.

'I rang the next number: they weren't home.'

Judy, normally good in a crisis, was beginning to panic. 'I'm taking my phone with me and rushing down and getting my uniform out of the laundry and trying to climb into it. It was an absolute farce because while I was on the phone I couldn't be climbing into my uniform, and when I was doing that I couldn't talk on the phone!

'The third house I called didn't answer either. It was a terrible situation, but I realised that I wouldn't be panicking if I was doing something constructive. I put the phone down, got dressed and went out the front door expecting to see all of the CFU unit out there working. Instead I saw numerous fire engines from the NSW Fire Brigade and realised the fire had got away and that from past experience they knew exactly where it was going to go.'

Encouraged, Judy started to get her head together. Her house is at the end of Merrilong Avenue on the side of the hill. Access is via a long, steep driveway, then steps lead to the staircase, which is two levels high. It's not easy, and new visitors are puffing if they try it too quickly. Judy started the trek down to the street and back again, which she undertook probably twenty times in the next few hours.

'I went to the neighbour's house, where there was a woman and her twenty-year-old son at home. I knew he had no training so I told him everything he had to do. He was looking shocked and wasn't old enough to be very responsible. But he just did everything I told him, and off I went.'

The rental property next to Judy's caught fire on the roofline, and the fire brigade were quickly on hand to douse the flames. Judy and other members of the CFU helped with the hoses along the firebreak, ferried water and messages, checked on neighbours and directed traffic.

A dozen or so fire brigade members arranged themselves in Judy's backyard, directing their hoses at the fire as it circled around the bottom of the street. Judy realised she had done no preparation inside her own home. A friend arrived to help, and she set him to work placing wet blankets under all the doors and windows and around the door of the garage. He arranged pots and buckets of water inside, in case the water went off and the fire wasn't contained, plugged the drainpipes and filled the gutters.

'It was forty-five degrees and terribly hot,' says Judy. 'We were taking turns at using the hose at the firefront. The fire brigade were making sure we all got to do this as well. We were trained. It was our first big test, and we wanted to participate.

'I think we could take on anything now.'

Because it was a Saturday, there were plenty of family members to call on. But if the fires had broken out during the week, Judy would have called on three or four other women in the street to do the fire hose and standpipe preparation. 'We would have coped,' she says.

'The people in our street were already a good community before the fires. We used to have street parties if anyone left or arrived. These CFU meetings were just an extension of that. And of course the fires have brought us closer together now.'

Fighting fires is mentally and physically exhausting, she says. 'I am reasonably fit, but we didn't stop working until eleven that night. The next day I was wandering around in my dressing gown, feeling stunned. And then at about eleven that morning I got a phone call from the fire brigade team leader saying, "We might be reactivated." Five minutes later, we were.'

A second very hot and windy day had followed and spot fires were flaring up throughout the park again. The CFU went back into action, rolling out the hoses, squirting property in preparation for the fire brigade. 'When the fire brigade arrived they helped us for a while, and when they thought we were reasonably under control they went away, leaving us in charge. They said that if everything got too big we should ring triple oh. We called the emergency number once more that day, but finally everything was okay.'

Judy now finds the park much more accessible with all the ground cover reduced to ash. She understands that fire is a natural part of the Australian landscape, particularly in the national park, but she was surprised by the damage caused by this fire. 'It's more like scorched earth,' she says. 'The bush will struggle for many years to recover from this.'

THIRTEEN

BURNING SUNDAY

Here is a foolproof way of putting your life and the lives of others in real peril.

Live in Australia, in steep country with beautiful views over national parks, surrounded by so many other people that the fire brigade is unable to supply one truck for every fifty homes. Live on a narrow, winding road preventing easy access and quick exit, with big trees planted everywhere, including in your garden.

If this is not risky enough, you can go further. Live in Australia in the middle of summer, during a drought, under water restrictions, among occasional visitors and holidaymakers who have no idea of the fire threat and no sense of community.

Make sure the area has low water pressure in a street where at least one house is surrounded by uncleared vegetation.

For real risk takers, other factors may be added. Live there on the hottest day on record, with strong winds forecast and with an even stronger wind change predicted for later in the day. Have no fire plan, make no bushfire preparations and go without an escape plan. And toss a coin for the final variable. Heads, an arsonist; tails, a careless machinery incident that creates sparks in dry scrub.

This is a scenario that confronts tens of thousands of people throughout Australia every year.

The beauty of the landscape, the peace of the Australian bush on a quiet summer's day, the glorious views attract people to these fire-prone locations. And these are the factors that brought Charles and Kathie Smith to Phegans Bay, across the tranquil Brisbane Water from Woy Woy, seventy kilometres north of the Sydney Harbour Bridge. They had arrived three months earlier from another of the world's fire-prone regions, Silicon Valley, California, where they had lived for the previous six years.

Charles grew up in regional New South Wales, but when he wanted to come home he and Kathie chose the New South Wales central coast. It is perhaps the most beautiful place in Australia. On one side are the steep tree-covered hills and ravines of the Brisbane Waters National Park, an extension of the Blue Mountains escarpment; on the other is the sparkle of views over inland and coastal waterways, and from some places the Pacific Ocean. All this is close to the amenities of a large city. Gosford and Woy Woy were once regional centres, with their own industries of shipbuilding and timber-cutting, but over the years Sydney has grown so large that they are almost outer suburbs.

Kathie and Charles lived with two of their three teenage children, Helen and Celeste, in a brick veneer two-storeyed house with a tiled roof at Wattle Crescent across the road from Brisbane Waters National Park. This park, and most of the surrounding backyards and streets, is dominated by fire-prone eucalypts, stringybarks and angophoras, the latter sometimes called Sydney red gum. Trees are very important in the area for both ecological and aesthetic reasons, and the Gosford Council has established firm guidelines for the preservation of the tree-rich lifestyle. Eucalypts and angophora cover the Brisbane Waters National Park in a seemingly continuous line to the water's edge. This is surprising, as the council's own website suggests this is a fire risk, advising residents to 'Ensure vegetation does not provide a path for the transfer of fire to the house.' The same website even describes the trees that are the biggest fire risks: 'Avoid plants with high levels of volatile oils in leaves – eucalypts, callistemons and melaleucas burst into flames on heating and increase fire intensity. In eucalypts the amount of volatile oil in foliage can be over 4 per cent, whereas conifers have up to 2 per cent and callistemons and melaleucas up to 1 per cent. Generally the figure is less than 1 per cent for acacias, grevilleas and hakeas. Introduced deciduous and evergreen hardwoods have the lowest amounts, with less than 0.1 per cent of volatile oils.'

It was a risk that most people were happy to live with, including the residents of Wattle Crescent. Most of the homes in this street are on large blocks, with a row of houses on even bigger blocks behind them. These were the first homes in the area and their gardens were overgrown. The eucalypts and angophoras in the backyards were enormous, overhanging several properties. It looked very beautiful.

Kathie, a film producer who describes herself as a 'city chick', was aware of the bushfire threat. 'It struck me when we bought here that the place was a fire risk,' she says. 'But the owner said there hadn't been any fires here in years and with all the neighbours around I felt we were in our comfort zone.' Wattle Crescent has a small dip in it, with Olive Avenue to the left; this street is about 200 metres long and ended at a row of houses overlooking the water. A small footpath ran off the end of the avenue down to the water, a further 300 metres down the hill. It's a hard hike up the hill from the water's edge, and the climb is even steeper from the other direction, to Woy Woy Road, the western boundary of the Brisbane Waters National Park. The skyline was dominated by a rocky, tree-covered ridge, beyond which was the 120-metre-wide F3 highway, with the park extending further beyond that to the west.

Kathie and Charles set about reducing the vegetation in their backyard, discovering problems when it came time to do something about three enormous angophoras with their high concentration of volatile oils. The difficulty is summed up on the Gosford City Council website: 'No person shall ringbark, cut down, top, lop, remove, injure or wilfully destroy any tree without council approval.' The Smiths and others in Phegans Bay discovered that the council does not make it easy to cut down the big trees. Charles and Kathie's neighbour and good friend, seventy-three-year-old Ray Bryant and his wife Jeanette, had been asking the council for years to clean up an adjoining block. Ray says: 'The neighbour never cleaned up, so the council sent some contractors around. They chopped everything back for about fifty centimetres from the edge of the fence, but they left all the debris on the ground. We knew we'd be in trouble if there was a fire.'

It's not as if bushfires are unknown in the region. They are, in fact, frequent and severe. This is the recent tally provided by the New South Wales Rural Fire Service:

1990/91 On December 23, hundreds of fires were reported across the state with eight emergency declarations made [in areas including Ku-ring-gai]. Eight homes were lost.

1991/92 On October 16 emergency declarations were made for the councils of Baulkham Hills, Gosford City, Wyong Shire and Lake Macquarie. Nearly 2500 bush firefighters battled more than 30 blazes around the state. 14 homes were destroyed.

1993/94 In late December 1993, a series of fires began on the north coast and in the Hunter region ... fire occurrence spread from the Queensland border to Batemans Bay [south of Wollongong]. At the height of the exercise over 20,000 firefighters were deployed, four lives were lost and 206 homes destroyed.

1997/98 There were major fires in the Burragorang, Pilliga, Hawkesbury, Hunter, Shoalhaven, Central Coast and Sydney's south ... that proved difficult to contain and suppress.

2001/02 The initial impact of seven 'Bushfire Emergencies' occurred during the period 29 October 2001 to 9 November 2001 in the areas of Cessnock, Gosford, Gloucester, Kempsey, Wyong, Greater Taree and Singleton.

On New Year's Day 2003, the authorities were prepared for fire. The NSW Rural Fire Service took the unprecedented step of issuing a 'pre-emptive action' warning for all its volunteer and professional units, putting them on duty for the following few days. It was the first time this kind of action had been taken on a large scale in New South Wales, but with forty-three-degree temperatures forecast and humidity in the low teens, the RFB was under no illusions about the fire threat: 'If new fires do break out tomorrow they will be extremely difficult for our firefighters to control.'

At about lunchtime on New Year's Day Charles, Kathie and Andrew, a friend from Canberra, were watching television downstairs. 'It was too hot to be upstairs,' says Charles. 'It was quiet. There were a lot of people away on holidays and those who usually come here during the holidays had not yet arrived.'

The fire threat arrived by a roundabout route. 'The power went off,' says Kathie. 'Charles and Andrew went out into the street and saw a few neighbours gathered around a single power pole.' They were looking at billowy white cumulonimbus clouds showing over the ridge and climbing up into the sky: the first telltale signs of fire.

Charles was in no doubt about the loss of electricity. 'We saw the smoke clouds over the hill behind us, about one or two kilometres away. It looked as if it was being fanned by northeasterly winds, which would take it away from us. A few people were laughing and they went away and got their cameras.' Kathie also got her video camera and started shooting. Some of the footage would later feature in her own film, *Burning Sunday*.

Then the wind changed, picked up and drove smoke into the faces of the watchers. Moments later, everybody saw flames licking at the treetops on the near side of the ridge: the fire had jumped the F3 and was charging at full speed towards Phegans Bay.

Charles saw the danger immediately. He said to everybody: 'Let's get back to our homes and get ready for this fire to hit us.' They had ten minutes before the ember attack, thirty minutes before the full fury of the fire front arrived. 'It was panic stations,' says Kathie. 'We were very unprepared for fire. Charles and I raced home, although for me it was more a panic run. I was thinking: What things should I be doing, and in what order?'

Andrew, who had fought fires during the Canberra blazes three years earlier, reminded everybody to change into fire-protective clothing. Charles found a heavy cotton shirt and sandshoes, Kathie went for jeans and hiking boots.

'We could see the fire approaching very quickly, and soon it would be all around us. I could see the flames coming through the trees. It was smoky, smelly, hot and very uncomfortable. I grabbed the two girls and two bags with papers, passports and important things that I had put aside in case of something like a house fire.'

A fire brigade vehicle raced into the street. Officers were telling residents to evacuate. The freeway was already blocked, so there was no exit that way. The remaining access would be needed for fire trucks.

Kathie says, 'Neighbours said they'd walk to the bay down Olive Avenue and meet there. The girls started to walk down and I planned to catch up with them a few minutes later. I grabbed towels and blankets, ready to soak them, and said to Charles, "We should evacuate."'

But Charles had no intention of going. He wanted to save his house.

With two neighbours and his friend Andrew, he formed a team to protect the street. 'We ignored the fire brigade. A lot of able-bodied men were evacuated, which I think was a mistake. In this street with ten homes only four of us stayed.

'It was in fact a very easy decision to make. We had a safe point as the middle of our street had no trees, so we could fall back, if the worst came to the worst, and one of my neighbours had a pool, so we could retreat to that away from major flames, if things turned cactus.'

By now the street was covered in eye-stinging gum tree smoke. The flames were only a matter of hundreds of metres away, fanned by strong winds. Embers were falling everywhere and starting spot fires immediately, especially on the lawns, which were dry because of water restrictions.

Flames were charging down the hill through the stringybarks and paperbarks and the open, tall angophoras. The main fire front was heading south towards Horsefield Bay, one of the first suburbs on the western edge of Woy Woy. But as the wind changed from the west, the fire flanks became the firefronts, and Phegans Bay was directly in their path. The Rural Fire Service deployed to the south, where they needed to make a stand to prevent the far larger number of houses at Horsefield Bay from being destroyed.

Phegans Bay Rural Fire Service unit was on 'property protection' and houses at Horsefield Bay were their first priority. The first building in the path towards Phegans Bay was the Rural Fire Service headquarters. The shed was empty because the unit had been deployed earlier, but eight cars belonging to volunteers were parked outside. The local unit couldn't respond to its own emergency, but the Wendoree unit was in the area. Captain Sacha Price arrived and ordered the hoses dragged out to see if they could halt the fires, now threatening the brigade building.

Seven of the vehicles parked outside the shed were alight, but there was nothing to be done. Twenty-one-year-old Ashleigh Crocker tried to rescue camera gear from his burning Pajero and was injured in the process. 'I got a lung full of smoke. It was like someone sitting on my chest,' he says. He was treated in hospital. His view was that: 'As long as no one dies, it's cool,' echoing the sentiments of most firefighters when they go into property protection mode.

Back at Wattle Crescent, Charles and Kathie were arguing about Charles's decision to stay. Kathie: 'I said, "It's only a house,

I think we should evacuate." He said no, he'd stay and meet us down the bay afterwards. I felt life was more important than property and the priority should be to save life. It was the worst possible time to have a disagreement because we hadn't discussed it before. Everything was on the spur of the moment.'

But Charles had a clear plan in his mind. 'I wanted to keep the embers away from the roof line of the home. We needed to stem the fire and keep the embers away from the angophoras. We knew we had to keep the flames away from the wooden fence. Then we had a buffer to my home, then to the neighbour's.'

What Charles did not know was that his neighbour Ray Bryant was asleep on his lounge next door. He had closed nearly all his windows and pulled the blinds down to prevent the oppressive heat getting in. He was totally unaware of what was happening outside. Charles had no idea he was there.

'We were pretty cool, calm and collected,' says Charles. 'About ten or fifteen minutes after they had spotted the flames at the top of the ridge the fires were throwing off embers that soared into the backyards and trees around the street. I wanted to get on the roof, get the hoses going, wet everything down. The roof was the best place to protect my home. The embers turned to constant sparks in the air. But the roof was a good place because I could act as a spotter for the people on the ground, as it had a good commanding position in the whole street. I was shouting and directing people to the embers with buckets and towels.'

Emergency authorities discourage this kind of behaviour, as it puts people in great danger.

'Three of us focused on keeping the fire out of the neighbour's yard, which was covered in tall shrubs and pine trees and angophoras. We filled the buckets and put full buckets of water on the fence at the rear to stop it from burning. It was best to use the buckets; water pressure was very low. Here at the top of the hill water pressure's a laugh at the best of time. We had six buckets of water in which we soaked about thirty towels, which we used to put out the embers and small fires.'

The flames were confined to the high side of Wattle Crescent. As Charles had noticed, the street was a natural firebreak. People had only to stop fire getting into their homes.

Charles was forced to sit down on the roof. 'It was extremely windy. I had the hose up there and filled the gutters and tried to keep things wet. Some of the roof tiles cracked under my feet as I walked on them, so I stayed on the apex. I saw the fire turn and go down what now looked like a natural fire course, when it reached the vacant block next to Ray's.' The angophoras on the vacant block which overshadowed Ray's house and cast embers into Charles's house burst into flame with an almighty roar. The firefront had arrived in the worst possible place at the worst possible time. Charles, watching from thirty metres away, was shaken: 'That was pretty scary.'

When the trees went up, Ray Bryant woke from his doze, slightly disoriented. The air-conditioner and radio were off, it was dark and there was a smell of smoke. 'I saw smoke coming into the laundry so I went to see what was going on.

'When I got there, I had the shock of my life. The whole backyard was on fire. I ran outside and grabbed the hose, but it had started to melt and stuck to my hand. I saw some fires break out in the mulch near the back door, so I picked up the nearest thing I had, a watering can, filled it at the tap and tried to pour it on the fires. But as soon as I had one fire out another would start.' Ray was quickly being overwhelmed.

'The smoke was black and thick and I had trouble breathing. The noise was enormous, like it was rolling out of a didgeridoo, only louder. I was yelling out: "Help! Help, someone! Charles! My house is on fire!" Charles couldn't hear me, even though he was only a few metres away, over the fence.

'Then I looked down the side of the house and saw that everything in the neighbour's block along the side of my house was on fire. The next door block had undergrowth that reached to the height of my eaves. The trees and shrubs were throwing flames as high as my house into my block.

'I looked into the sky and saw more flames coming towards me. I tried to get more water, but the heat was terrible. I started to panic, and in about half a minute I gave it all up. Darren, our neighbour from across the road came in and told me he thought

I'd better get out of the place. I wasn't really in any state to hang around.

'I got the car and reversed down the street and there were some kids with dogs standing there. I gave them a lift, and we all went down to the sea. For the next four or five hours I had real trouble breathing. My eyes got hurt and have been sore ever since.

'My wife was with our relatives at Gilgandra. One of the grandchildren saw the fires on the TV news and said, "Nanna, that's your house on fire."'

Kathie Smith had decided that she would do what she could to protect their house, though she was still determined to leave. 'I made sure everyone had water, gave them towels, put blankets under the doors and windows. Then Charles said, "You should go now."' The priority was the girls.

Kathie went into the street and came across a bunch of red-faced, crying or screaming children. 'At that point there were embers everywhere, and the children were red and hot and panicking. Where there are kids in trouble, it really does focus me. I put wet towels over their heads, which protected them, cooled them down and stopped them from screaming.

'Ray came out of his house next door, picked up the children and their dogs and drove down the hill with them.'

Up on the roof, Charles was nervous about his decision to stay with the house. 'I was on my roof, thirty metres away from the trees, when the big trees went up. They didn't just catch alight, they actually exploded. There was a blast of air that knocked me back three metres on my roof, and I fell over. It was as if I had been showered with fire. I was a good distance away, but thank God I was on the apex. It would have blown me over the edge.

'When that happened, Ray's house caught fire. There was nothing we could do.

'Because the house next door was starting to catch fire, I realised I had to try and protect the small wooden pergola on the fence line to my house. Which reminded me that we had two gas bottles connected to the house on that side. I was extremely tense but thought my home would survive: I had done everything I could. I could choose to leave if I wished. I was reasonably calm, my friend and neighbours were around me, and we kept our heads.'

Kathie thinks that most other people in the street had lost theirs. 'It was pandemonium. I was very worried, but Charles and Andy were experienced, they'd been through bushfires before. They had transport, and I knew that if they were in trouble they could have come down to the bay. At the time there were no fire trucks, it was just the neighbours going round in cars, trying to find a way out of the street. But the roads up the hills were all closed.

'I followed the girls down to the bay, but I didn't find them: I spent about fifteen minutes looking, getting a bit frantic. Then one of the neighbours said they had probably been evacuated by the fishermen.' In fact that day 200 people, including the Smiths' daughters, were taken to evacuation centres by an armada of fishing boats. The fishermen had done this before.

Kathie could have gone with the next boat, but she was worried about Charles and Andrew. She returned home. 'It was absolutely black, smoky, choking, I had difficulty breathing. I had a coat around my head. I could hear the fire crackling in the distance and the wind roaring, pushing the fire on. I looked over the hill and saw fire in the street, on the ridge, and I thought all the houses in the street were on fire.

'There were embers flying everywhere, but now there was a fire truck out the front of my house.'

Sacha Price's Wendoree unit had arrived, and the first thing they did was to pour water on the gas bottles and between the Smiths' house and that of Ray next door. Unfortunately, Ray's house was now on fire. Sacha says: 'We can't put out a house that's fully on fire.

'We have no breathing apparatus and can't go inside, and anyway the house roof was fully alight and was threatening to fall in. Gas cylinders don't usually explode unless they are leaking or unless there is something wrong with them, but we poured water on them and the walls, just to be safe.' They poured water over the bottles for an hour and a half: Ray's house caught fire at the side, then the second storey, then the lower parts and finally the front.

Sacha had been working on fires near Phegans Bay for two hours. 'I've been a fire volunteer since I was seventeen, but this fire was different for me. It was the first time I'd seen a house burn down with everything inside since I bought my own home. My husband was at home with our five-month-old daughter Kayla, and I knew they could see other fires closer to home. I started to wonder whether they were safe.'

Kathie was traumatised by the fire, exhausted by the heat and the steep walk to the water and back, worried about Ray, her children and her possessions. 'The doors to our home had been opened to let the fire brigade through to the backyard, so there was a foot or so of smoke coming down from the ceiling. It was choking. There was some fire damage to the back of the house.

'I felt utter devastation. Suddenly your security is gone. It's a bit like walking on a bridge and the bridge collapses under you and you fall into the chasm below.'

The firefront passed. 'I was very red at this point and my body temperature was up. I had a bath and got changed and then went over to the neighbour's house and sat there for thirty minutes and did nothing.'

Charles and the neighbours still had plenty of work to do. 'I stayed on my roof for four or five hours, telling the team to put embers out,' says Charles. 'There was a massive amount of leaf litter still burning and embers. We had a little time to think about water and food, and to find out what had happened to the rest of the family.

'I knew Kathie had gone across the road and my daughters had evacuated to the waterside, and there had been a little Dunkirk happening down there. Kathie reappeared out of the smoke from across the road with a wet towel over her head, and we regrouped for two hours.'

The fire that passed over Wattle Crescent destroyed Ray's house and a part-finished house on the vacant block next door. Other houses in nearby streets were razed. The fire continued down the hill but was no longer burning so fiercely – until the wind changed again and pushed it up again.

Fires travel faster uphill. This one didn't have a lot left to burn, but the house across the road from the Smiths was made of brick, and it had a massive angophora out the back, spreading its branches across the roof.

Charles says: 'There was a huge threat from that angophora. It was night now so the flames looked more intense. The fire brigade poured an enormous amount of water on that tree, but it just wouldn't stop burning for hours. We patrolled the street all night, putting out embers. Every house seemed to have pine bark for mulch, so we had to go from house to house throughout the night putting neighbours' fires out.'

The next day the Premier of New South Wales and the media turned up and the place became a circus for twenty-four hours.

People who wanted to grieve and be together found their privacy being invaded: a few still resent the government for that.

Charles believes the actions of his little team saved the street from much greater devastation. 'Our team of four people bought the fire brigade thirty minutes. If they hadn't come after half an hour then I think our house and the one across the street would have gone. They were really stretched. We bought them time to deal with the fires in other streets, and move the front line back one street. They were here for eight to twelve hours, dousing spot flames and keeping the gas bottles cool. The firefighters were exhausted by that stage.'

Sacha Price is still the crew captain. Charles and Kathie sent her a picture of herself in the street, which she thought was a lovely gesture. 'The firies were great, but they have about thirty trucks for hundreds of houses in dozens of streets. They couldn't do it all. We had to help,' says Charles.

He remembers what he saw while Ray's house was burning down. A second-storey picture window overlooked his house, and he could see it from the roof. He could see the flames taking hold in the ceiling upstairs; the whole interior turned orange. Set in the window was a figurine showing the head and shoulders of a woman. Charles thought it was a child's toy, but in any event it is etched into his memory. It defined for him the things that are permanent and precious, all of which can be lost so quickly in a fire.

Kathie remains astonished by the courage of the volunteers and their determination to stay for however long it took.

Next door Ray and Jeanette Bryant rebuilt their home. It looks fireproof, but they know that a lot depends on the preparation of the whole community. Ray, who knows he could have been burned to death that day, remains philosophical about it all. 'Someone was looking after me,' he says. 'I wish he would look after my golf handicap too.'

ACKNOWLEDGMENTS

The people who agreed to talk about the most terrifying moments in their lives did so in the hope that others reading this book will benefit from their experience. Some of the recollections are deeply personal, and I am grateful I was invited to share the memories of these difficult and emotional periods in their lives. None of the people in this book believes their actions were perfect, none believes they were acting heroically. They just confronted the difficulties in the best way they knew how, and they wanted to keep their families safe.

Emergency agencies understand that people are not always prepared for the psychological impact of bushfires; and all have encouraged me to write this book in the hope that it will help a little. All agencies have cooperated fully and supported my research in an open and welcoming way, particularly the South Australia Country Fire Service, The Country Fire Authority of Victoria, The Tasmania Fire Service and The NSW Fire Brigades.

Understanding human motivation is vital when trying to ask the right questions to produce a book like this. Thanks to Professor John Handmer (RMIT University) for his insights and encouragement. The book *Disaster Resilience: An integrated approach* by Douglas Paton and David Johnston was useful, as was *Promoting Community Resilience in Disasters* by Kevin Ronan and David Johnston. Justin Leonard of CSIRO was generous with his time discussing fire physics.

Thanks to Bruce Esplin, Naomi Brown and John Gledhill for their advice and encouragement.

The book owes a great deal to the work of Phil Ashley-Brown of ABC Local Radio who started the process with his great audio series *Bushfire*.